soft dough

crazy dough

buckwheat

Camargue

Libertarian

Bagging machine

Neroli oil

Innovation

mill

chambell's girl

miller

baker

pastry-maker

salesperson

dough cutter-cum-beater

Elisa test

big-bag

French rice center

sticky

coumarine

Syracuse

Nathaniel Doboin
and Thomas Teffri-Chambelland

Gluten-Free Baking

Photography: **Louis Laurent Grandadam**
Text: **Chae Rin Vincent**
Preface: **Alain Ducasse**
Tasting and recipe decoding: **Steve L. Kaplan**
Translation: text, **Flo Brutton**;
recipes, **Anne McDowall**

Éditions
de La Martinière

Contents

Preface

The beauty of the *Chambelland* story lies in its simplicity: the story of two young men who followed their dream and quietly embarked on a mission to change engrained habits. It is also a powerfully human story, proving that we can change the way we eat and the way we produce food. But let's start at the beginning.

I first met Thomas Teffri-Chambelland and his associate Nathaniel Doboin in early 2014, a few months before the opening of their bakery in the Village Popincourt, a small village-like neighborhood in the heart of Paris. Thomas was by no means a newcomer to the business, having already opened two organic bakeries: La Paline in Sisteron and La Fabrique à Pain in Aix-en-Provence. He was also the founder of the international bakery school near Sisteron (2005), with extensive experience of consultancy in France and abroad. For this first meeting, he brought along three different types of bread for me to sample: his "village bread," an "athletes' bread," and a 5-grain bread. One taste was enough to prove his case. The crumb had a deliciously natural flavor—buttery, with a slightly moist chewiness in perfect contrast to the crispy crust. Who needs cake, I thought, when you can have breads like these? And with that, I decided to serve them in my restaurant at the Plaza Athénée hotel in Paris. I had a special breadbox made that slices the rectangles loaves into perfect rectangles, which we then serve with free-range butter as a prelude to the meal.

But this is no ordinary bread. This is bread made from rice flour–and that's a real tour de force in technical terms. Though relatively unknown in the West, rice flour has been around since ancient times in the East, where they use it to make rice paper and rice noodles (to give just two examples). The common factor is rice-flour dough, which unlike its wheat or rye-based counterparts, doesn't rise. It doesn't rise because rice is a gluten-free grain, and gluten is what captures the carbon dioxide released in fermentation and makes a dough rise. Without gluten, making good bread is quite a challenge and it took every ounce of Thomas's experience as a former biology teacher to make it work. Having reinvented himself as a baker to pursue his passion, he ultimately reinvented the staff of life itself. But our story doesn't end there. The lessons to be learned from this adventure reach far beyond one man's well-deserved success story.

Thomas and Nathaniel soon realized that they couldn't grind their rice in just any grain mill. It had to be a mill exclusively reserved for rice to avoid the risk, however small, of gluten sneaking into the mix. So they joined forces with miller Stéphane Pichard and built a mill of their own–in Malijai some 20 miles from Sisteron in the valley of the Durance. I hear they now have plans to grow their own rice too, which is not so surprising when you remember the wheat fields that Thomas has already planted around his bakery school near Sisteron, so his students can better understand how flour is made.

Traceability from grain to bread–that's what matters to Thomas and Nathaniel. And as the producers of organic, gluten-free bread, supply chain traceability matters even more to them than to their counterparts in conventional farming. Because only supply chain traceability can guarantee quality control from start to finish. That's where the story of our two young men goes beyond the boundaries of their personal adventure and sets an example for others to follow. Their story may be modest, but it lays down a legacy that reaches far and wide.

Economics, technology and agriculture, taste and health–all of these dimensions come together here to tell a bigger story. Good food–meaning food that does you good and tastes good–is only as good as its ingredients, which in turn depend on planet-friendly farming practices and the very highest standards of food processing. As this book shows, technology and hedonism can be friends, and it is possible to change the way we produce our food. Imagine a world where dozens of people like Thomas and Nathaniel are committed to making their dreams happen. A world flowering with the myriad initiatives of women and men determined to restore the connection between plate and planet–with *Chambelland* bread as their emblem.

Alain Ducasse

Foreword

People often say to us, "You're so lucky to do what you do and lead such a project."

But what exactly do we do? The answer is a bit of everything rolled into one: milling, research, baking, selling and management. That's what gets us out of bed every morning, knowing that our life is filled with the things we actually want to do.

What's lucky is the chance we have here to explore new ways of being—new ways of thinking and acting that will make yourself and others happy. The key is feeling free to express yourself and rice certainly offers us plenty of room for self-expression. Rice drives everything we do on a daily basis. It is the signature element of those products that are now proudly displayed on the walls of our baking hall of fame, taking its place alongside wheat and rye.

This book gives us the perfect opportunity to share our convictions as entrepreneurs—our belief in organic farming and a form of farming that brings together people and talents to build a sustainable industry.
That's why we only use a variety of organic rice that comes direct from the producers, Gianmario Viola and Laura and Livia. It's also why we built our own mill from scratch in partnership with Stéphane Pichard, to be sure of producing high-quality, naturally gluten-free flours suitable for bread making without the use of preservatives or additives. What you have in the end is a harmonious blend of skills, each one a link in a value chain held together by generosity and the love of a job well done.
Within these few pages we try to give an idea of the particular strengths of these skills. We also hope to explain why we attach such importance to the quality of our raw material—and with that in mind, we take you on a tour of our production areas, in Lombardy, the Alpes-de-Haute-Provence department and Paris.
The end of the book features a collection of recipes to try at home so you can share the *Chambelland* adventure, among them recipes signed by chefs we work with every day—because we wanted them to speak for themselves. May they be a further source of inspiration for your experiments in baking, pastry-making and cooking in its widest sense.

Bon voyage and happy tasting!

Nathaniel Doboin
& Thomas Teffri-Chambelland
Co-founders of Chambelland

(earl grey, jasmin, menthe,
lapsang souchong,
genmaicha, rooibos, verveine)

jus de fruits bouteille   3,5/
limonades bouteille   3,5/
eaux minérales bouteille   3/3

7/7,7 €   jus frais maison   4,5/

Chambelland is a fine adventure story about two young entrepreneurs who decided to make bread with rice. Two free thinkers, Nathaniel Doboin and Thomas Teffri-Chambelland, who set out to build a bridge between France's rich tradition of baking and something truly innovative. Their dream was to focus on rice as the key to a food innovation that would transform a naturally gluten-free product into something delicious.

Achieving that dream has meant building a whole new industry at the service of a noble raw material. It has meant building a mill exclusively reserved for one type of flour. In short, it has meant rethinking everything to come up with a *different* take on bread. Even the shape has changed. *Chambelland* loaves are shaped like books.

The shape says it all. Behind the shop window of the *Chambelland* boulangerie on the Rue Ternaux are shelves laden with loaves as enticing as unopened novels. Every one has a story to tell. So let's step inside and listen to what they have to say.

CHAMBELLAND-
SELECTED
JAPONICA RICE

A meeting

The story of *Chambelland* really began with a meeting between two men, Nathaniel Doboin and Thomas Teffri-Chambelland.

Nathaniel Doboin, though born in Paris, grew up in the countryside, at the foot of the Luberon mountains. He cut his professional teeth in Chicago, then in Paris; he was crazy about traveling, the movies' and photography. He embarked on a career in photography and got swept up in the frenzied life of an advertising producer–a formative experience for our young artist, but one that too often left him feeling adrift. So he quit his job to travel the world with his partner Gaëlle, and give some direction to his life.

Two years later he returned to France and explored the possibility of retraining. All those years of business school could surely be put to another, more personal use. What he most wanted to do was launch into something he felt passionate about, a life that made sense and also helped him to help others.

"After two years of backpacking around the world I wanted to do something firmly rooted in everyday reality, something directly related to meeting basic human needs such as food and sleep."

Thomas Teffri-Chambelland was also born in Paris and also moved to the South of France as a child. He started his career as a biology teacher but quickly realized that the French education system was too conservative for a man of his entrepreneurial aspirations. What he wanted was an adventure that would free his creative spirit, and bread making–which he had learned from a girlfriend while a student at Marseilles University–fitted the bill perfectly. It was a eureka moment. He would become a baker. So he signed up for a CAP (diploma in professional baking) and henceforth spent his days teaching and his evenings studying baking in his kitchen. On graduating, he learned the ropes in a collective bakery on a biodynamic farm where quality mattered more than baking traditions.

This is where he opens his own bakery, La Paline, named after the small board used to place the bread on the baker's peel. He specializes in *pain biologique au levain* (organic sourdough bread). Very soon he moves his little business to premises dating from the 12th century, newly restored by Thomas and wife Hélène, in the historic center of Sisteron.

In the beginning he bakes one batch of bread a week, which he only sells at the local market.

"Those first few years we lived like bohemians! It was a new approach, selling extra-large, five or six pound loaves by weight. The mere fact that our bread wasn't round or shaped but more typical of regional bread (*pain de Lodève*, for instance) flouted the rules of classic bread baking."

Thomas became such a success that fellow enthusiasts came calling to find out about organic sourdough bread. By 2011 Thomas was ready to open his own school: the Ecole Internationale de Boulangerie (international bakery school) in Noyers-sur-Jabron, Alpes-de-Haute-Provence department.

Nathaniel and Thomas met a year later, Nathaniel hungry for new endeavors and Thomas nurturing an idea just begging to blossom. And so began the *Chambelland* adventure, born of an encounter between two determined entrepreneurs who would form a long-lasting friendship. As Nathaniel puts it:

"Today, we're more like brothers than friends, so close that working together every day takes on a whole new dimension. There's a real intimacy between us."

When the time comes for big decisions, choices that will determine the future of the business, our two friends go hiking in the mountains to clear their minds–their version of "summit meetings," says an enthusiastic Thomas:

"nothing but the mountains beneath our feet, a backpack and a water bottle."

It's outings like these, and traveling as a pair to places like Italy, the USA, and even Japan, that give shape to *Chambelland*, honing its identity as an enterprise that combines passion, innovation and tradition.

Chambelland, so charming!

When Nathaniel and Thomas decided to open a bakery focused on rice-flour bread, it was their idea that the emerging market for gluten-free foods was ready for some bold innovation.

With this in mind, Nathaniel paid a visit to that cradle of new food trends, California, where he found a dynamic market driven by easygoing businesses. "Even though production standards weren't always up to the mark, it was enough to persuade me that we could indeed create a warm and welcoming bakery offering gluten-free breads that weren't simply aimed at tackling health issues. From that point forward, wellbeing and pleasure were our watchwords."

And why the name "Chambelland"? That too, says Nathaniel, was inspired by his trip to California. "I was at a farmers' market in Los Angeles talking to a producer and happened to mention that we were thinking of starting a new bakery. Sounds interesting, he said. What were we going to call it? I was lost for an answer—neither Thomas nor I had given this any thought. But thinking of Thomas, I came out with 'CHAMBELLAND'! *'Chambeland,'* he said, pronounced the American way. 'So French! So charming!' It was an instant hit."

And with that, the bakery had its name. In retrospect, it makes obvious sense. As Nathaniel points out: "To French ears, the *'chamb'* in Chambelland sounds like *champs*, meaning fields. And cultivation is a key factor in our thinking about rice production. Then there is the *Grand Chambelland*, the keeper of the keys to the king's bedchamber, his trusted confidant. The way people with gluten intolerance need to trust that they are not being tricked into eating gluten without knowing it."

Traditions versus innovations

Traditions were important for Thomas and Nathaniel but so too was envisaging the future. So they thought long and hard about the type of bread they wanted to make, starting with the most basic question of all:

"What is bread?"

In France, bread generally means baguette, a symbol of national identity and one third of that inseparable triad (to a French person at least): baguette, wine, and cheese. But though baguette is certainly bread, not all bread is baguette. French ethnocentricity aside, bread comes in a multitude of shapes and sizes depending on where you are in the world. There is pita, naan, vollkornbrot, lavash, chapatti, ciabatta–what else is this if not bread?

So Thomas and Nathaniel went back to the origins of bread, the universal bread recipe:

flour + water + baking

Technically speaking, bread is a combination of flour and water that's left to ferment (in most cases) then cooked.

After that the permutations are endless, it's all a question of imagination. Your classic baguette is made from wheat flour; Portuguese *broa de milho* and Mexican tortilla are made from corn flour; and Central European black bread is made from rye flour. So why not get creative with rice flour? Why not indeed, thought our two entrepreneurs, and rice flour it was. Making bread from rice flour met all their requirements.

They could indulge their taste for tradition but with an offbeat twist–rice–to come up with real bread products that were naturally gluten-free into the bargain. It was a perfect combination of tradition, innovation, and forward thinking.

Chambelland offered consumers a whole new take on bread, though as Thomas points out:

> "Baking didn't wait for us to come along. The history of baking dates back millennia, as does its symbolic importance. To make any sense at all, *Chambelland* bread had to take its cue from traditional baking, using a sourdough starter. We don't pretend to have reinvented baking–merely to have combined our fascination with rice with our love of bread. The rest is down to technique."

It's a bit like walking a tightrope, adds Nathaniel:

> "with tradition on one side and innovation on the other, without ever taking sides. Accepting what is and letting go."

31

In keeping with time-honored practice, *Chambelland* bread plays around with shapes and cooking methods. Square breads, flat breads, bread rolls, bread baked in traditional rotary hearth furnaces, bread baked in ventilated ovens– inspiration abounds for those who open their eyes to the world. Looking beyond French borders, Chinese *mantou* are steamed, Indian chapattis and Mexican tortillas are roasted on a hot plate, Mongolian boortsog are deep fried ... at *Chambelland*, the innovations just keep on coming.

Rice: the grain of the future

When Thomas and Nathaniel chose rice as their raw material, they were fully aware of the social implications of their decision.

Bread has been a staple food around the world for centuries. In France, bread is affordable to everyone and rooted in daily routines. At the global level, rice provides more than 20% of all calorie intake and is the main ingredient of the cuisines of South America, China, India, Japan and many more besides. According to the statistics hub Statista, global rice consumption continues to increase, rising from approximately 437 million metric tonnes in 2008 to 477 million metric tonnes today. In India, the cultivation and domestication of rice dates back to c. 1500 BC.

European rice paddies, on the other hand, are a much later phenomenon. Italy quickly established itself as the number one rice producer in Western Europe, profiting from the foresight of the Cistercian monks who first introduced rice to Italy in the 12th century. Another great boon for Italian rice cultivation were the irrigation systems designed by Leonardo da Vinci, most notably in the Lombardy region. The Italian Piedmont is meanwhile famous for its production of Carnaroli and Arborio rice, the main medium-grain varieties used in risotto. These two regions are now considered the rice bowl of Europe, their flat expanses of green gold extending across clay-rich soils generously watered by the Po River.

Rice was pretty much the obvious choice, says Thomas, partly for price reasons and partly for reasons of food ecology.

"Technically speaking we could have gone with another gluten-free grain such as quinoa, teff or amaranth. Except that the price per kilo is steep and they have a bigger carbon footprint due to their distant production zones. It's true that rice trades at three times the price of wheat but it can be grown locally and even organically at a price reasonable enough to keep our bread affordable."

Rice makes it possible to meet one of the biggest challenges of the 21st century: how to eat well on a low budget without stinting on flavor. For Thomas and Nathaniel, food should always be a pleasure and *Chambelland* bread—a dense, half white, half brown sourdough rice bread with a low glycemic index—is a perfect demonstration of a nutrient-dense food that is also packed with taste.

Bread making with rice flour

Who ever heard of rice-flour bread? Not our first customers, that's for sure. But if they found the absence of baguettes surprising, that was nothing compared to the discovery that *Chambelland* was a "rice-bread only" bakery.

It is certainly not approved practice in France to make bread with rice flour—no more than it is to make square loaves. French bread is typically round, the most obvious example being *pain boule*. None of this counted for our free-spirited Thomas Teffri-Chambelland who firmly believes that "even the most widely held beliefs should be questioned."

Never one to turn down a challenge, Thomas built on his existing skills and came up with a new line of bakery products. Rice offered the twofold advantage of being an innovative cereal that was also naturally gluten-free. But his plan could only work if people accepted the idea of a rice-based bread—and if he could bake gluten-free products that tasted good. That was Thomas's cue to conduct his own experiments, or in the words of the man himself:

> "Venture into the imagination, be creative, intuitive, awaken my senses."

Working with a new cereal was admittedly a tall order. As Thomas says, "every cereal imposes specific constraints that must be obeyed." First comes understanding your raw materials: "becoming so familiar with your grains that you know exactly how they will react to cooking." Everything starts with the rice grain itself. "For me it's all about working intuitively, about immersing yourself in a cereal and coming to know your grains—their world, their cultivation, and their behavior in milling.

"I did a lot of background research, most notably through the French rice center, which we still use for analysis and bread-testing purposes."

Along the way, Thomas devised recipes and thought up ways of working with rice to bring out its goodness and magnify its qualities. Moving from thought to action was what took the longest.

"Once an idea had matured, I would put it to the test—which in the end took very little time because I knew by then what to expect. If I didn't get the results I wanted, I knew I had to think again."

Rice is filling, nutritious, and tasty; it is also easy to grow, stably priced, and naturally gluten-free into the bargain. And no one knew better than Thomas just how much his unassuming little grains had to offer.

So what delicious bakery products could he make with rice? Wheat can be turned into baguettes and croissants but what new goodies could rice deliver? For Nathaniel and Thomas, one thing was certain: there was "no question of creating substitute products. Your baguette contains gluten, which is as it should be since without gluten the flavor and texture of baguette is bound to disappoint. Instead, we came up with a range of products that take account of the characteristics of rice—its mouth-feel and subtle, vanilla-like aroma of tonka bean."

Being creative and constructive is what *Chambelland* is all about. As Nathaniel sees it, "bread making with rice flour enriches traditional baking by introducing a new tasting experience aimed at meeting the demands of the modern consumer." With that in mind, Thomas set about producing an array of bakery products based on gluten-free recipes that he had been working on for the past ten years: focaccias, *pissaladières* (Provencal pizzas), muffins, *chouquettes* (bite-size choux puffs), and even his very own version of sugar bread!

New cereal, new recipes, new tastes .... Taste in particular was the number one consideration for our *Chambelland* bakers, but this being gluten-free bread, they had to find a way of making a light and airy crumb without the help of gluten. For Nathaniel, the idea was to create bread that "everyone would want to eat, not some foodie remedy." That meant rethinking traditional baking practice in search of a new approach geared toward a new type of flour.

Rice bread is naturally devoid of those gluten proteins that give structure to baked goods and retain the carbon dioxide produced in fermentation. So Thomas developed a new method of making dough rise that would exploit the characteristics of their chosen grain while showcasing its superior quality.
Therein lies the secret of those crusty creations with the melt-in-the-mouth crumb on display in the *Chambelland* store window.

Square loaves in fine shape

At *Chambelland*, it isn't just the flour that's unconventional, it's also the shape of the bread itself. Behind that tempting window display in Paris's Rue Ternaux are sleek, shallow, square and rectangular loaves that are a far cry from the "boule": the round-shaped bread for which the *boulanger* is named.

As with the name Chambelland, there is a story behind these strangely shaped breads. It dates back to the days before the boutique in Paris's 11th arrondissement when Thomas and Nathaniel were commissioned by the International Federation for Human Rights to supply the bread for a congress held at the Paris City Hall. With 500 guests in attendance, it was a golden opportunity to unveil their rice-flour bread, remembers Thomas. "We'd always gone for a rectangular shape focused more on crust than crumb but we'd never actually put it to the test." In the event, their passion paid off: "our long slices of bread and butter got a resounding thumbs-up from everyone present!"

Once they'd decided on the shape, the next step was to create the baking molds—custom-made molds, designed to exact specifications for breads that resemble fine books. Stepping into the *Chambelland* bakery is like stepping into a delicious bookstore where every loaf has its own eloquence: *pain de village*, thick crust, silky crumb, voicing aromas of rice and buckwheat as nature intended; *cinq grains*, flourishing a crust dotted with five different seeds, poppy, sesame, sunflower, and gold and brown flax seeds; *pain des athlètes* expressing figs, apricots, and hazelnuts. Every story has its heroes, and this one—soft, crisp, and unforgettable—is no exception.

The art of slicing

How should we define *Chambelland* bread? As a big and beautiful book weighing four and a half pounds–clean lines, rectangular shape, resolutely modern and innovative. So innovative in fact that it didn't fit a conventional bread slicer, which posed a real problem in terms of retail sales. It was Hélène, Thomas's wife, who came up with the solution: a breadbox cum slicer, inspired by the cabinet-making techniques she learned as a student at the Ecole Boulle (college of fine art and crafts in Paris).

The result is an elegant box that cuts the whole loaf into halves then quarters. To extend the book metaphor that so perfectly describes *Chambelland*, customers are free to pick whatever takes their fancy: grimoire, large format, or paperback.

A custom-made slicer for custom-made bread was perfectly in tune with the spirit of *Chambelland*–a lyrical, poetic spirit that attracts the attention of passers-by in the Rue Terneaux as they glance inside the store, and see the bread being sliced.

The industry. From rice grain to rice bread

Bread is so much part of everyday life that hardly anyone ever thinks about the origin of the flour used to make it. When Thomas and Nathaniel decided to launch *Chambelland*, one of their first questions was where their raw materials would come from. The French wheat industry had been well established for decades but the rice industry had to be built from scratch.

They tried using organic rice from the Camargue, France's only rice region, but the results were not convincing. Camargue rice producers deliver the total volume of their freshly picked crop to rice brokers or collection points, which invariably stock the rice in silos regardless of the differences between varieties. What *Chambelland* needed were pure-line, selected varieties of consistent quality and in sufficient quantity.

At this point in our story, it is some years since Thomas's bakery school in Sisteron began working with a miller called Stéphane Pichard, from Malijai, in the Alpes-de-Haute-Provence department. It was Stéphane who put the *Chambelland* team in touch with Gianmario Viola, a cereal grower and trader based in northern Italy, who in turn introduced them to Lombardy rice farmers Laura and Livia, who are *Chambelland*'s suppliers today. The fact that the rice doesn't come from French rice fields makes no difference in terms of the carbon emissions owed to transport.

Gradually, an organic rice farming industry began to take shape, drawing on the abilities of skilled workers of both sexes who together make up the ramified *Chambelland* network. For Nathaniel and Thomas, building an industry depends on building trust and keeping that trust alive. This is why, three times a year, Nathaniel, Stéphane, and Thomas make a point of paying a visit to Laura and Gianmario, one a rice farmer, the other a grower-trader, both of them guarantors of the quality of *Chambelland* bread. It is thanks to their painstaking work that these precious grains of rice exist at all, to be ground in

LIVIA'S FARM

the *Chambelland* mill, then made into the bread that graces the shelves of the boulangerie in the Rue Terneaux, baked on the premises by proud owners Thomas and Nathaniel.

The cycle of rice, grown in Italy by Laura and Gianmario

> "Vaï vaï! Don't worry, I drive down here all the time!"
> "Sé… sécura ?"
> "Si ! Vaï ! Vaï ! TRANQUILO!"

The words are those of Laura and Gianmario. We are standing at the top of a talus slope leading to the last rice plot harvested by Laura: he looking worried at the wheel of his vehicle even though it's an SUV; she growing increasingly impatient as she tries to reassure him. Petite and soft-spoken Laura may be, but her voice packs a punch.

Welcome to Cascina Fontanina, in the village of Lomello, about 40 miles to the southwest of Milan. Since 1998 Laura has farmed this 42-hectare organic holding singlehanded, specializing in the cultivation of rice and corn plus a small percentage of field beans, a nitrogen-fixing green manure. Nearly half of her land goes to produce 140 metric tonnes of rice per annum, including the rice destined for the *Chambelland* mill.

But then, this is Lombardy, which together with Piedmont is considered the rice bowl of Italy. Rice has been growing here since the 15th century, blessed with abundant sunshine and watered by a network of inland water sources (the River Po and its tributaries) that make Italy the leading producer of European rice.

LAURA
ON HER TRACTOR

51

It is early October and the rice growth cycle is nearing its peak at the Cascina Fontanina. The seeds are sown in April in dry soils then continue to grow throughout the summer season, the fields being progressively flooded to compensate for the heat stress caused by the extreme temperature differences between night and day. Water here plays a vital role in providing a kind of "thermal blanket."

As harvest time draws near in September/October, plots bordered by talus slopes are drained of their water via a system of makeshift sluices: wooden panels along the edges of the plots, which are raised to let the water run out. Rudimentary but remarkably efficient.

Laura's lands being located north of the Po, her main problem is maintaining a balanced water supply while keeping to the supply times allotted to each grower. Here as elsewhere, water is a shared responsibility.

Paddy stubble is all that remains on the last field harvested by Laura, waiting to be turned into compost and plowed back into the soil. The crops are planted on a rotating basis so next year this same field will be planted to corn, not rice.

For just over a week now, our rice-farming signora has spent four hours a day at the wheel of her combine harvester, her petite silhouette in striking contrast to the impressive proportions of the machine. Straight after harvesting the rice is passed through a sieve to eliminate any impurities, followed by a heavy-duty drier that removes any residual moisture liable to ferment the grains. When thoroughly dried, the rice is stored for three months in two silos, each with a capacity of 75 metric tonnes, before being sold to a grain trader.

THOMAS AND LIVIA
IN THE RICE GRANARY

For the past 15 years, that person has been fourth-generation farmer Gianmario, an early player in the trading of organic raw materials including soya, rice, wheat, and corn. Since the early nineties, Gianmario has steadily built up a network of some 240 farmers, mainly concentrated in the Piedmont and Lombardy regions.

On arrival at his works in Voghera, some 40 miles south of Milan, the rice is hulled between rubber rollers to remove the outer protective shell and bran layers. As Gianmario explains, talking nineteen to the dozen: "The bran is used for chicken coop bedding, while the inner rice grains are whitened between grinding wheels—and the faster the grinding, the less the risk of damage to the rice. It's not like with wheat. Lastly the grains are passed through an optical sorting machine that removes any unripe, green grains."

A percentage of the rice is then transported to the *Chambelland* mill in the Alpes-de-Haute-Provence department.

In terms of quantity, *Chambelland* may be small fry for a trader like Gianmario, but that doesn't make Nathaniel and Thomas's project any less attractive. He got to hear of them through Stéphane, the miller on the team, and has supplied the mill since 1995. It's a relationship built on trust, a mutual confidence that is there for all to see. "That's what organic food is all about," insists Gianmario. "A relationship founded on trust, not just business and trade."

As if to prove the point, after saying his goodbyes to Laura, Gianmario shows us his own crop of rice—a first for this wry fifty-year-old, but a move very much in line with the libertarian ethos of *Chambelland*. "If my father were alive today, he'd say I'd gone mad growing rice here, south of the Po. Doing something new simply isn't in the nature of peasant stock like us.

"But me, I believe in what rice farmers are doing around here. Partly because in years to come the other side of the Po is in for big environmental problems due to the heavy metals from industrial wastewater; and partly because the idea of growing so-called 'non-traditional' crops really appeals to me. I guess you could call me an altruist!"

Growing his own rice crop posed a real challenge to our rice trader:

"This side of the River Po, pollution isn't a problem. The water for my own lands comes out of the ground beneath my feet, so I don't depend on the irrigation canals. No, the problem here is extracting water from clay soils. North of the Po, where Laura is, they have the opposite problem—retaining water in sandy soils."

In the event, his gamble has paid off handsomely, his three-hectare plot yielding 24 metric tonnes of rice. Next year he fully intends to make this nine hectares, rising to 40 hectares within three years.

GIANMARIO'S
RICE GRANARY

At the *Chambelland* mill, in Malijai, with Stéphane Pichard

A sustainable supply of rice was certainly an important factor for the *Chambelland* team, but it wasn't everything. The industry they had in mind also depended on a painstaking rice-milling process that would deliver flour of a consistent quality, and do so what's more in a truly gluten-free environment.

When Thomas and Nathaniel embarked on this project they knew little or nothing about rice growing and even less about milling. Stéphane Pichard, on the other hand, comes from a family of millers spanning six generations and had been supplying the bakery in Sisteron for several years. He was born into the flour business.

Thomas and Nathaniel had found their man! All they had to do now was sell him on the idea.

A miller and a mill

"When Thomas tapped me on the shoulder and asked me to join them, my answer was: NO WAY!

"I had enough on my plate running the Pichard mill, which produces 3,000 metric tonnes of organic flour per annum", says Stéphane with a smile. But Thomas didn't give up that easily. So eventually "no" turned into "maybe"; and with a bit more coaxing from Thomas, "maybe" turned into "yes."

"Let's do it! Let's build this mill!"

61

But then, entrepreneurship comes naturally to Stéphane, a craftsman who loves everything about his job and became a miller despite his father's hopes of a better life for his son. "From the moment I started training as a miller in 1988, I was interested in every aspect of flour production, from wheat crushing to sales of finished product. Walking the land with farmers looking for the best suppliers of cereals, inventing flour recipes—I enjoyed it all."

By 1992 he had bought a mill of his own, in Malijai, on the outskirts of Bléone, in the Alpes-de-Haute-Provence department. Today he crafts a range of artisan flours exclusively made from organically grown wheat and spelt.

Organic production was non-negotiable for *Chambelland* but to guarantee that their flour was free of gluten their rice had to be milled in an environment uncontaminated by any other cereal. For Thomas and Nathaniel there was only one thing for it: they would build their own mill, close to Stéphane's milling works in the Malijai business park, with Stéphane as joint manager. "Build" here has to be understood in the sense of assembling the milling machine, not constructing the building itself.

A colossal assembly puzzle

So Thomas, Nathaniel, and Stéphane set off to find the machine of their dreams—which they eventually found in Italy. In early 2014, two semi-trailer trucks arrived at Malijai loaded with what looked like the parts of a giant Meccano set, and nothing for instructions except a diagram scrawled on a sheet of A4. Three months and a colossal assembly puzzle later, Stéphane and Thomas, assisted by a boilermaker and millwright, had managed to make the machine fit the mill building. If that brings to mind lyrical images of windmills, waterwheels, and millstreams, think again. This is a purpose-built, steel-structure warehouse, with state-of-the-art production and storage facilities.

May 2014 saw the first sacks of flour roll off the production line. With a crushing capacity of one metric tonne per hour, the mill can operate continuously for five days out of seven. But let's not overstate the case, says Stéphane. "The volumes we handle here are a mere drop in the ocean compared to the big producers. And with an annual output of 300 metric tonnes of flour, we are still a long way from running at maximum capacity."

Guided tour

Stéphane takes us to the mill storage facility where the rice is delivered on arrival from Italy. "We're talking about organic, whole grain rice that has been cleaned and sorted. Not broken rice because you can't trace the varietal identity of broken rice. Ours is what's called "cargo rice," meaning whole grain rice with the outer layer, the "husk," removed, but retaining the bran and germ layers.
"At *Chambelland* we typically handle small volumes, double-checking everything along the way.

> The cereals are stored in 1,000-kg bags, at a temperature not exceeding 14 °C (57 °F) to avoid the risk of oxidative rancidity."

A sample of each batch of the raw material is sent for analysis to test for gluten contamination, and suitability for bread production. The same goes for the flour when the time comes. "So if ever there were a problem," says our guide, "we would know exactly at what stage it occurred. The contaminated batch would be withdrawn and the machines

65

cleaned to eliminate all trace of gluten. So far there hasn't been a single instance of contamination since the mill opened; all of our samples, rice and flour alike, have tested negative for gluten."

The sound of machines tells us we're nearing the heart of the action: an area of some 3,000 sq ft, where the grains of rice are fed through a series of fluted mill rollers, before being run through a sieving machine to produce a fine-grained, even-textured flour.

The finished product finds its way to the ovens of the *Chambelland* bakery at number 14, Rue Terneaux, but also to other bakeries and mills wanting to try out new products based on shelf-stable, naturally gluten-free flours containing no additives.

Among these professionals are new converts to gluten-free baking. Stéphane admits that until a few years ago, he had always found gluten-free artisan bread something of a disappointment. That changed with the opening of the *Chambelland* bakery. Tasting their bread, he says, was a revelation: "It was surprisingly good. That was the day I realized that it is in fact perfectly possible to make gluten-free bread that everyone will want to eat."

"Today, I make my living as a rice farmer, like my father before me 30 years ago when he blazed a trail for organic farming."

The Village Popincourt, home of the *boulangerie Chambelland*

Number 14, Rue Ternaux, in Paris's 11th arrondissement. The somber façade of the *Chambelland* bakery looks onto a spacious terrace brightened by colorful furniture. Here, as in certain small market towns in Italy, no one bats an eye to see keys come flying out of windows, or children playing ball while their parents relax on the sidewalk nibbling something delicious. A village square, neighborhood life, echoes of former times bustling with haberdashers, upholsterers, and couturiers clustered around a covered market. Understated elegance meets local buzz.

For Nathaniel and Thomas, Paris's Village Popincourt had exactly the right feel for their bakery. As Nathaniel puts it, "It had to be somewhere with soul, a place that spoke the same language as *Chambelland*." It was months before they found it but when they did, says Nathaniel, "it was love at first sight."

Breakfast time these days sees customers take their places around tables outside and inside the bakery, or in the case of *Chambelland* habitués, order directly at the counter–*chambelline*, slice of *cinq grains*, whatever takes their fancy. In the basement meanwhile, bakers are kept busy baking.

Because behind this fine display of breads and pâtisseries are dedicated artisans making dough, filling bread molds, and keeping an eye on the ovens. Every day, from 3 o'clock in the morning till the store closes at night, bakers, pastry-makers, and salesmen toil away behind the scenes, catering to the taste buds of Village Popincourt aficionados.

chambelland propose

humeur du jour

commandes au comptoir

e Bonheur est un voyage et mon une destination...

majoration de 10% appliquée à toute consommation sur place

plat rappo souri hollywood

boissons certifiés AB

Prix emporter / sur place

espresso, allongé	2/2,2 €	chocolat épicé maison
cappuccino	4,5/5 €	jus detox maison 4,5
noisette	2,2/2,4 €	(citron, gingembre,
latte, latte soja	3/3,3/3,5/ 3,9 €	herbes aromatiques, miel)
thés & infusions	4,5/5 €	citronnade maison'été
(earl grey, jasmin, menthe,		jus de fruits bouteille 3,5
lapsang souchong,		limonades bouteille 3,5
genmaicha, rooibos, verveine)		eaux minérales bouteille 3/

6/6,6 €   sandwich végétarien   7/7,7 €   jus frais maison   4,5/

The major stages of bread making

Bread making

Warning

The recipes that we invite you to try in the second part of the book start with the skills that every good baker has at their fingertips. Because mastering the art of baking—finding just the right mix of technique, sensibility, manual dexterity, and kitchen-tech savvy—takes years of experience. Being an intuitive cook helps, but it's just the beginning. All of which is to say that the results you obtain at home may not match those obtained by an artisan baker armed with just the right tools for the job.

A few basic principles

To get started in baking, you need to be fluent in the basics: a few golden rules that once understood will allow you to make any kind of bread you choose.

BASIC BREAD DOUGH

There are four things to keep in mind when making bread: the proteins and sugars present in the flour, the water, and the yeasts.

When wheat flour is mixed with water to make dough, the protein–or glutens–in the flour form a springy, water-insoluble mesh of fine, coiled strands.

Meanwhile, the yeasts (single-celled microorganisms) feed on the sugars in the wheat flour starch, releasing bubbles of gas that are held fast by the springy gluten substance, helping the dough to rise.

Once fully risen, the dough is ready to go into the oven.

Baking firms up the texture of the dough, producing bread.

GLUTEN-FREE BREAD DOUGH

As we have just seen, wheat flour protein–gluten–is essential to form the water-insoluble mesh that traps the bubbles of gas released by the yeasts. Without that water-insoluble substance, there is nothing to stop the bubbles from escaping, so the dough doesn't rise. One of the challenges of making gluten-free bread is to find another way of retaining the gas: make a dough that is viscous enough to trap the bubbles. Think of viscosity as the thickness of a fluid. If you use a straw to blow air into water, the bubbles disappear because water is too "thin" to retain them. But use a thicker, more viscous fluid like honey, wallpaper paste, or molasses, and the bubbles hang around for a while. The same would be true if you used white sauce or confectioner's custard.

Gluten-free bread dough must likewise be viscous enough to trap the fermentation gas that makes bread rise. Many gluten-free flours have a naturally high viscosity when mixed with water, buckwheat and chickpea flour for instance. Rice, corn and chestnut flour, on the other hand, have next to zero viscosity.

So to make good bread from low viscosity flours, we need to add natural thickeners such as carob seed flour, guar gum, or flax seed gum.

Rice

Rice originated in South East Asia where it has been cultivated for more than 10,000 years and is now grown on every continent on Earth except Antarctica.

Asia remains the world's leading producer of rice, with Italy as the leading European producer. French rice production is meanwhile concentrated in the Camargue region.

There are thousands of different varieties of rice, which are classified according to the characteristic of the grain: whether round grain, long grain or extra-long grain; sticky, colored or scented rice.

Freshly harvested rice, known as "paddy," is enclosed in an outer layer called the hull or husk. "Cargo rice" refers to whole grain rice with this outer layer removed, but retaining the bran and germ layers.

White rice is milled rice that has had the bran and germ removed.

Corn

The ancestry of this cereal can be traced back thousands of years to the Mexican plateau, where corn, or maize, was the staple food of the native Americans.

At the end of the 15th century, Spanish navigators brought corn to the Old World where its cultivation quickly spread.

These days corn is grown on every continent, except Antarctica. It is the most widely cultivated cereal on the planet, with the United States as the world's largest producer. In France, corn is the second most widely cultivated cereal, essentially concentrated in southwest France, Brittany, Alsace, and the Pays de la Loire region.

Corn, high in starch and rich in oil, is mainly grown for animal feed; but sweet corn is usually grown for human consumption, as kernels, corn on the cob, semolina, corn flakes, starch, and, of course, flour.

Buckwheat

Buckwheat, despite the name, is not related to wheat and is actually not a cereal at all but a flowering plant with pyramid-shaped fruits called achenes. It is believed to have originated in northeastern Asia and is mainly grown in Asia and central Europe as a source of fiber and plant-based protein. In France, buckwheat is usually found growing in low fertility soils, typically in Brittany and the Auvergne region.

Chickpea

Chickpeas, or garbanzo beans, are legumes that originated in the Near East and are now grown on every continent except Antarctica. They have become a staple food in India, which is now the largest producer of chickpeas in the world. In France, chickpeas are mainly cultivated in the south of the country where dry soils provide ideal growing conditions. Chickpeas come in thousands of different varieties, depending on the size and color of the chickpea, which ranges from light to dark brown. High in plant-based protein, chickpeas are a particular favorite with non-meat eaters.

Chestnut

The chestnut originated in the temperate regions of Asia Minor and Europe and is now mainly grown in Asia (China, South Korea, and Japan) and Mediterranean countries, most notably Turkey, Italy, and Portugal. In France, chestnut production is mainly concentrated in the departments of the Ardèche, Dordogne, and Lozère. Chestnuts long remained the staple ingredient of the traditional diet in rural Europe, earning the tree its sobriquet of "bread tree." But chestnut production plummeted in the 19th century due to something called "ink disease" (chestnut blight fungus), which devastated chestnut groves. Chestnut flour is a specialty flour made from dried and ground chestnuts.

Flours	Rice	Corn	Buckwheat	Chickpeas
Plant family	Cereal	Cereal	Fruit of a flowering plant	Legume
Growing region	Every continent except Antarctica, but mainly in Asia. Italy is the number one European producer. French rice production is concentrated in the Camargue region.	The most widely produced cereal in the world, with the USA as the world's largest producer and France as the largest European producer.	Mainly grown in Asia and Central Europe. French buckwheat production is concentrated in Brittany and the Auvergne region.	Mainly grown in India but also in Australia and Mediterranean countries. French production is concentrated in the South of France.
Taste	Neutral, subtle.	Naturally sweet, with a soft flavor.	Nutty.	Subtly sweet, takes on a roasted flavor when cooked with sugar, vanilla or coconut.
Physical characteristics	- Fine, light texture. - High in starch so useful as a sauce thickener. - Crumbly texture ideal for crumbles. - Adds crunch, particularly to breadcrumbs. - Can be mixed with other flours for a rounder, fuller flavor.	- Yellow color, adds golden tones to food - Useful as a sauce thickener. - Can be used alone, or mixed with a food starch such as potato starch for a more airy texture.	- Gray, speckled black color, darkens the color of food. - Dense texture with a strong taste that begs to be mixed with more neutral-flavored flours, and food starches that add lightness.	- Pale yellow color. - Dense, packed texture—can be mixed with food starches for more airy results.
Recipes	Asian pastries (eg coconut pearls, Japanese *daifuku mochi*), rice noodles, Chinese dumplings ….	Mexican tortillas, American cornbread, Portuguese *Broa de Milho* (cornbread), Basque *talos* (corn pancakes), *Gaudes Bressanes* (cornmeal porridge from Bresse) ….	Brittany *galettes* and *kig ha farz* (buckwheat pancakes and dumplings), Japanese soba noodles, *blinis* (Russian pancakes), couscous and *Crozets Savoyards* (small, square flat-shaped pasta from the Savoie region).	Indian *socca* (flatbread), *panisse* (fritters), *pakoras* (vegetable patties) *besan puda* (chickpea flour crêpes), Sicilian *panelles* (chickpea fritters), Algerian *Kalantika* (chickpea pie).

Thickening agents

Most thickeners are naturally occurring, plant-based substances. Many are basic raw materials, including some that have been around since ancient times. Carob seed flour, for instance, has long been used to add creaminess to recipes. Other thickeners are the products of industrial chemistry. A good example is E464A (Hydroxypropylmethylcellulose), a modified cellulose mainly made from cotton by-products. *Chambelland* bread, as you would expect, is exclusively made using organically sourced, naturally occurring plant-based thickeners.

GUAR GUM POWDER

Guar gum powder is a traditional thickener obtained from the guar plant, a legume native to West Africa. It has a yellowish white color and a neutral taste and is versatile enough for use in hot and cold recipes alike. One of the strongest natural thickeners, guar gum forms a viscous gel when mixed with cold water that creates a feeling of fullness when eaten.

The guar, or "cluster bean," is mainly grown in India.

CAROB SEED FLOUR

The carob tree is native to the Mediterranean region and is one of the oldest trees in the world. It belongs to the legume family and is characterized by long, flat pods containing bean-like seeds, which are ground into a white, neutral-tasting flour.

Carob seed flour, though certainly a thickener, is relatively modest in effect. It is typically used to thicken ice cream, adding creaminess and improving melting resistance.

Spain, Morocco, and Italy are the largest producers of carob.

PSYLLIUM HUSK

Psyllium husk is used to add viscosity to gluten-free bread. It comes from blond plantain, or ispaghula, a herb native to India, with tiny seeds whose tegument (seed coat) contains mucilage: a plant substance that swells prodigiously in water to form a gelatinous mass. Psyllium has been used for centuries as a traditional remedy for sluggish bowels but its use in food is more recent. Psyllium husk powder works as a thickener and a binder while also adding chewy texture.

India is the largest producer of psyllium husk.

FLAX SEEDS

Flax is one of the oldest cultivated crops in the world. Flax fiber, obtained from the stem, is used to make fabrics while the seeds go to make linseed oil or are eaten just as they are.

Flax seeds are oval, flat-shaped seeds and come in two colors, brown or golden, both being equally high in fiber and Omega-3 fatty acids.

Once ground and mixed with liquid, flax seeds absorb water, producing a gelatinous substance that's useful when making gluten-free bread.

Canada is the world's largest producer of flax seeds, followed by China and the United States.

CHIA SEEDS

Chia is a flowering plant of the Salvia genus, originating in Mexico where it was cultivated for its seeds by the native Americans. Chia seeds are tiny, white, gray or brown seeds with a neutral taste, which expand in water to form a thick, gelatinous substance.

They are high in protein and fiber but rarely used in bread making, being mainly used to thicken smoothies and desserts.

Chia production is concentrated in South America.

Bread baking

Baking is the complex process that gives structure to dough, by turning up the heat to temperatures ranging from 100°C to 300°C (212°F - 572°F) depending on the type of bread. Heat causes the fermentation gas to expand, increasing the volume of the dough.

Adding steam to the oven before baking is essential for the loaf to rise to its full potential. The difference in temperature between the raw dough and the oven condenses the steam to water on the dough surface, preventing it from drying out into a crust and allowing it to expand before hardening off.

Another thing that happens in baking is the Maillard reaction: the caramelization of the sugars on the surface of the loaf that gives the crust its color and distinctive flavors, contributing to the character of the bread.

Bread staling

Soon after a loaf has been taken out of the oven and left to cool on a wire rack, deterioration inexorably commences. The crust loses its crunch, the crumb loses its moistness and the loaf turns stale.

Over time the water from the component with the highest water activity (the crumb) migrates into the component with the lowest activity (the crust). Hence the dry crumb and soggy crust.

Staleness occurs because the starch chains dispersed in baking realign and retrograde—what's known as starch retrogradation.

Wrapping the bread in a dishtowel or paper will help to retain moisture by reducing water evaporation. But it will also soften the crust, reduce the crunch, and hasten the staling process.

A *Chambelland* bread tasting
by Steven L. Kaplan

Simon-Nicolas-Henri Linguet, French lawyer and philosopher at the time of the Enlightenment, accused bread of being a "poison" that embodied the tyranny of grain. Rice was among the alternatives he recommended, for social not medical reasons, though almost certainly because he himself was gluten intolerant. But he would have been appalled at the idea of eating rice in the form of bread.

Linguet's contemporary and adversary, Antoine-Augustin Parmentier, chemist, moralist, and reformer, devoted much of his life to the study of bread, particularly the functions of gluten. Tasked with rendering the potato palatable as a famine food surrogate, he had to overcome the disdain reserved for it as a lowly food for pigs. To make it psychologically "good" to eat, he imagined casting it in the familiar, reassuring, quasi-sacred form of bread.

Two and half centuries later, controversy still rages over the definition of bread, not least over the seeming oxymoron "gluten-free bread."
Which brings us to the peculiar case of the *Chambelland* founders: two men marked by the solid traditions of French baking, who conceived a bread that defies convention (by removing gluten from the mix) but is based on traditional criteria in terms of process (a long, slow, gentle fermentation, the source of all taste and aroma) and results (the multiple qualities that engage all five senses).

So with those five senses in mind, let us now taste *Chambelland* bread, with the same rigor and enthusiasm we usually reserve for fine wine.

Their "foundational" loaf is the *Pain du Village*, an "organic" bread signifying that it possesses health benefits, among other things, not any particular sensorial distinction. It consists of 90% rice, the most widely consumed cereal in the world, and 10% buckwheat (which despite the name is not related to wheat at all, but is actually a fruit seed kindred to sorrel and rhubarb). An unlikely couple, rice and buckwheat, but it works well in physio-chemical terms by facilitating the production of bread without gluten without detracting from its appeal to the senses (appearance, crust, crumb, mouthfeel, aroma, and taste). Not exalting to behold, not quite two inches high, so hardly risen at all, the *Village* beguiles nevertheless with a tonic frankness, a straightforward property, just the trace of a smile scored in a crisscross pattern (like the steps of a polka) framed in a form resembling a squat house, rustic and rectangular, with a roof colored burnt-sienna and a façade in grayish-brown.

For a loaf baked in a mold, the crust is surprisingly convincing: more sonorous than crispy, delicate, not too crunchy, responsive to the touch, and well structured.

The *Village* crumb is not any more classical in type than its crust, but it is interesting, welcoming, in its way fetching–compact, with a tender, moist, sensual yet slightly sticky texture somewhat redolent of

Japanese *mochi*. Despite its density, there is nothing stifling about this crumb which projects a certain airiness or jauntiness, thanks to the inscription in its brownish, fleshy core of endless little holes of different sizes.

This cogent symbiosis of crust and crumb, moistened with the liquid sunshine imparted by olive oil, gives the bread a pleasant mouthfeel, yielding yet agreeably chewy. This propitious first impression leads us to the cardinal criteria of sensory evaluation: smell and aroma, and taste and flavor.

On the nose and palate, *Pain du Village* emits scents and aromas of a grilled toastiness that bring out the tension between two tones, one veering toward floral softness, the other slightly piquant, a tad spicy, almost peppery. I also detected notes of popcorn, dried apricots, autumn leaves, chestnuts, and freshly picked tobacco. Taken together, these create a composite flavor in which it is difficult to distinguish sharply the aroma from the taste. So we discern hazelnuts in a creamy sauce (more porridgy than milky), peaches, roasted notes, and a touch of tomatoes and mozzarella on the finish.

All in all, *Village* is an exceptional product. The paradox of gluten-free "bread" lies precisely in its dogged (and necessary) rejection of the very nature of conventional bread, while asserting its status as bread. What counts in the end is less its exotic character than its delicious essence. It goes well with a vast array of different foods. Articulated in three other versions, the *Village* launches us on a veritable sensorial odyssey.

The *pain aux cinq grains* is more visually striking than *the Village,* its rustic nature made more emphatic by a graphically engraved scoring, an earthy color imparted by good baking and "garden" effects that jump out at you.

The crust is sonorous-sounding and crisp to the touch, as if extending an invitation to discover viscerally the innards of the loaf. As in all conventional loaves seasoned with seeds (particularly when they are soaked and toasted), the flavor is heavily dominated by the interplay of flax, sunflower, poppy, and sesame seeds. A gusty whiff of almond partially eclipses the fragrance of toast. Muscular notes of fruit on the approach (pear and hazelnut, a hint of honey) gradually make way for a touch of pumpkin, followed by an impression of walnut salad. Provided one chews well, the mouthfeel is charming, the seeds slipping down nicely with the help of the olive oil.

Just as seeds supply the dominant flavor in *Aux cinq grains,* so a slightly tart chocolate inflects the *Pain au cacao* marked by a thick, voluptuous seam of chocolate that gives the bread an irresistible, cake-like look, with generous wisps of chocolate feeding through the crust. The palate, however, is neither long nor explosive, the chocolate effect being somewhat tempered by the "village bread" texture. The global sense is a less-than-seamless blend of rice, buckwheat, and cocoa. The cocoa bouquet is pleasing without being overpowering. The mouthfeel is slightly sticky and more refractory compared to the two previous loaves.

The *Pain des Athlètes*, the last of our samples, is not so much symphonic as playful: a bread overflowing with energy and enthusiasm, its crumb packed with huge chunks of figs and hazelnuts, which break through the crust in places to leave crater-like dents that make one think of the surface of the moon. Fruit dominates the palate. On the nose, the figs add a decidedly Eastern touch, evoking Corinthian currants and hints of pepper and apricots playing out against a backdrop of hazelnuts and toast. Like its chocolate counterpart, the *Pain des Athlètes* delivers richness with every bite—delicious on any occasion and particularly ideal as an energy-boosting snack or a bracing start to the day.

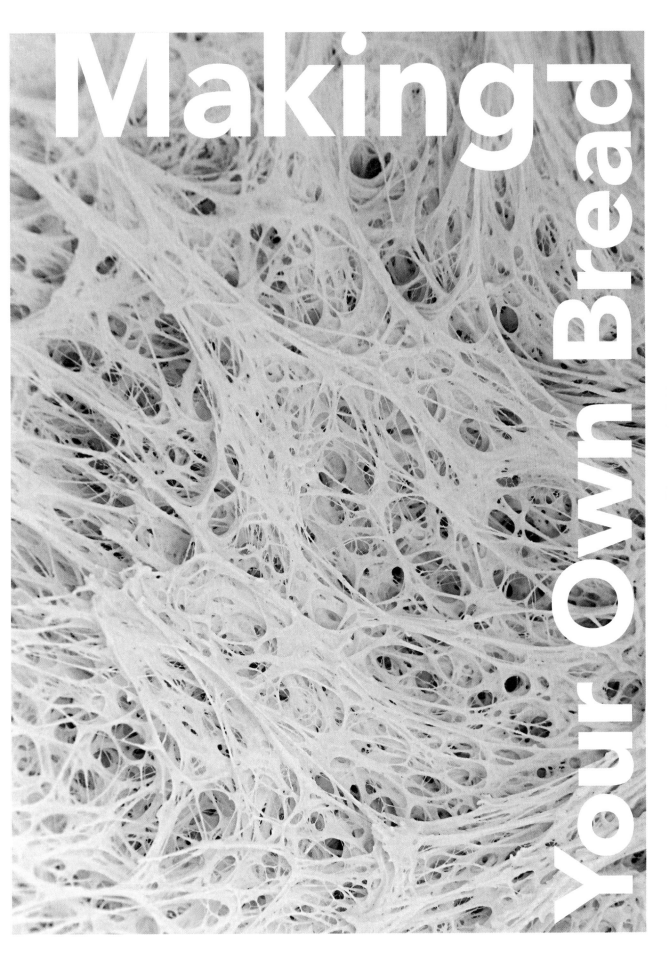

Making

g

Your Own Bread

GRAY MIX

5 ⅔ cups (2 lb/900 g) whole-wheat rice flour
¾ cup + 1 ½ tablespoons (3 ½ oz/100 g)
buckwheat flour
4 teaspoons (12 g) psyllium

YELLOW MIX

5 ⅔ cups (2 lb/900 g) whole-wheat rice flour
½ cup + 1 tablespoon (1 ¾ oz/50 g)
chickpea (garbanzo) flour
⅓ cup (1 ¾ oz/50 g) potato starch
4 teaspoons (12 g) psyllium
¾ teaspoon (2 g) guar gum

Preparing the Flour Blends

To make it easier to create the different recipes, you can use bread mixes made by the *Chambelland* mill or prepare these blends at home. If you make your own, we recommend you do so in advance.

We offer blends of gray or yellow flour, depending on your tastes.

Pour all the ingredients into the bowl of a food processor fitted with the paddle attachment and pulse at low speed for 5 minutes to obtain a consistent blend.
Store the flour blends in metal containers or paper bags, in a cool dry place, or in the refrigerator for up to two months.

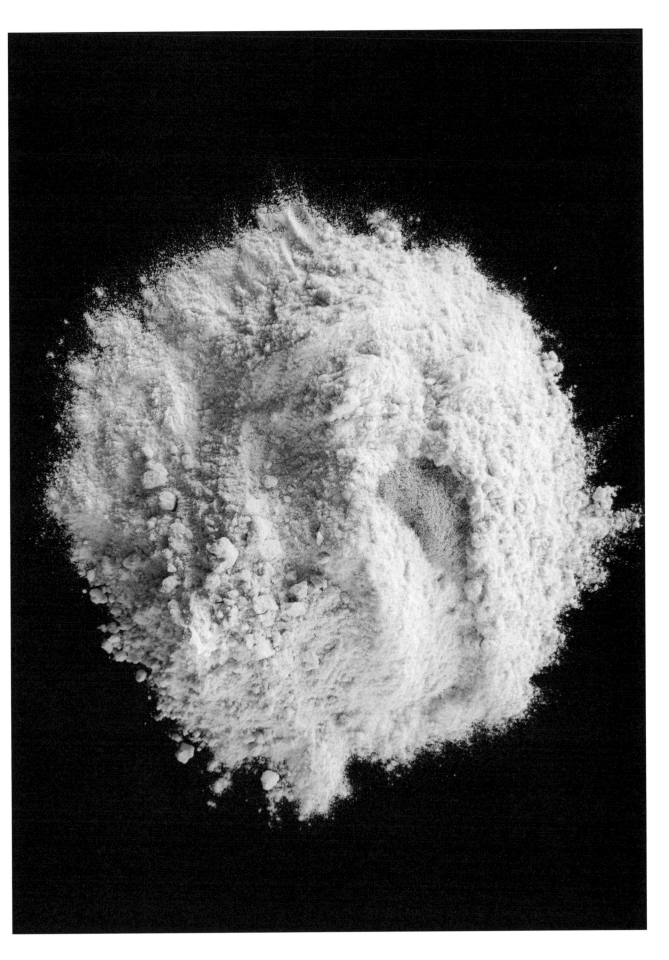

MAKES 1 X 1 LB 2 OZ (500 G) LOAF

Prep time: 15 minutes
Cooking time: 40 to 50 minutes
Proving time: 1 hour 15 minutes

You will need: 4 ¼-cup (1-litre)
nonstick cake pan

INGREDIENTS

2 cups (10 ½ oz/300 g) *Chambelland*
bread mix or gray or yellow flour blend,
as desired (see page 88)
1 ½ teaspoons fine salt
1 ¼ cups (300 ml) water at 100°F (38°C)
1 ¼ teaspoons (4 g) fresh baker's yeast
1 teaspoon olive oil
Oil for the mold

French Sourdough

Pour the flour, salt, and water into the bowl of a food processor fitted with the paddle attachment. Pulse at low speed for 10 minutes.

Add the crumbled fresh yeast and continue kneading for 2 minutes.

Pour in the olive oil and knead for a further 2 minutes.

Photo 1: Fresh yeast.

Photo 2: Incorporate the olive oil.

Photo 3: At the end of kneading, the dough should be smooth, with a thick bechamel consistency.

Photo 4: Counterexamples of a dough that is too firm and one that is too moist.

Photo 5: Place the dough into a nonstick mold or one that has been very lightly brushed with oil. Leave to prove for 1 hour 15 minutes at room temperature in a draft-free place.

Photo 6: The dough is ready to be placed in the oven.

Photo 7: Dust the top of the loaf with a little buckwheat flour.

Photo 8: Score the dough lightly using a razor blade.

Bake at 475°F (240°C) for 20 minutes, then lower the temperature to 390°F (200°C) and bake for a further 20 to 30 minutes, depending on your oven.

The crust of your bread should be golden. If you have a probe, check that the core temperature is above 205°F (96°C).

Leave the bread to cool on a wire rack.

Photo 9: The sliced baked bread, revealing its honeycomb structure.

Fragile dough needs to mature quickly, which can be achieved by using 100°F (38°C) water.

MAKES 1 X 1 LB 2 OZ (500 G) LOAF

Prep time: 15 minutes
Cooking time: 40 to 50 minutes
Proving time: 1 hour 15 minutes

You will need: 4 ¼-cup (1-litre)
nonstick cake pan

INGREDIENTS

2 ½ cups (10 ½ oz/300 g) buckwheat flour
1 ½ teaspoons fine salt
1 cup (250 ml) water at 100°F (38°C)
1 ¼ teaspoons (4 g) fresh baker's yeast
¼ cup (¾ oz/20 g) buckwheat flakes
for finishing
Oil for the mold

Buckwheat Bread

Pour the flour, salt, and water into the bowl of a food processor fitted with the paddle attachment. Pulse at low speed for 10 minutes.

Add the crumbled fresh yeast and continue kneading for 2 minutes.

Place the dough into a nonstick mold, or one brushed very lightly with oil.

Cover with a clean kitchen towel (without it touching the dough) and leave to prove for 1 hour 15 minutes at room temperature in a draft-free place.

Preheat the oven to 475°F (240°C).

Sprinkle the buckwheat flakes on top of the loaf, then score it lightly with a razor blade.

Bake for 20 minutes, then lower the temperature to 390°F (200°C) and bake for a further 20 to 30 minutes, depending on your oven.

The crust of your bread should be golden. If you have a probe, check that the core temperature is above 205°F (96°C).

Leave the bread to cool on a wire rack.

MAKES 1 X 1 LB 6 OZ (620 G) LOAF

Prep time: 15 minutes
Cooking time: 40 to 50 minutes
Proving time: 1 hour 15 minutes

You will need: 4 ¼-cup (1-litre)
nonstick cake pan

INGREDIENTS

14 oz (400 g) bread mix with seeds
or French sourdough ingredients
(see page 90)
⅔ cup (3 ½ oz/100 g) mixed seeds
(flax, sunflower, poppy, sesame, pumpkin)
Oil for the mold

Multigrain Bread

Soak ½ cup (2 ¾ oz/80 g) of the seed mixture in 4 teaspoons (20 ml) of cold water. Set aside the remainder of the seeds.
Follow the method for French sourdough (see page 90).
After incorporating the yeast, add the soaked seeds and stir in for 1 to 2 minutes, until you have a smooth dough.
Place the dough into a mold, or one brushed very lightly with oil.
Leave to prove for 1 hour 15 minutes at room temperature in a draft-free place.

Preheat the oven to 475°F (240°C).
Sprinkle the remaining 2 tablespoons (¾ oz/20 g) seeds over the top of the loaf.
Bake for 20 minutes, then lower the temperature to 390°F (200°C) and bake for a further 20 to 30 minutes, depending on your oven.

The crust of your bread should be golden and the seeds on the top toasted.
If you have a probe, check that the core temperature is above 205°F (96°C).

Leave the bread to cool on a wire rack.

MAKES 1 X 1 LB 2 OZ (500 G) LOAF

Prep time: 15 minutes
Cooking time: 40 to 50 minutes
Proving time: 1 hour 15 minutes

You will need: 4 ¼-cup (1-litre)
nonstick cake pan

INGREDIENTS

2 cups (10 ½ oz/300 g) *Chambelland*
bread mix or gray flour blend (see page 88)
1 ½ teaspoons fine salt
1 ¼ cups (300 ml) water at 100°F (38°C)
1 ¼ teaspoons (4 g) fresh baker's yeast
1 teaspoon olive oil
Zest of 2 organic lemons
¼ teaspoon fennel seeds, crushed
2 lemon slices
Oil for the mold

Syracuse Bread

Pour the flour, salt, and water into the bowl of a food processor fitted with the dough-hook attachment. Knead at low speed for 10 minutes.

Add the crumbled fresh yeast and continue kneading for 2 minutes.

Stir in the olive oil, lemon zest, and fennel seeds. Continue kneading for 2 minutes.

Place the dough into a nonstick mold, or one brushed very lightly with oil.

Place the two lemon slices on top of the loaf.

Leave to prove for 1 hour 15 minutes at room temperature in a draft-free place.

Preheat the oven to 475°F (240°C).

Bake for 20 minutes, then lower the temperature to 390°F (200°C) and bake for a further 20 to 30 minutes, depending on your oven.

The crust of your bread should be golden and the lemon slices starting to brown. If you have a probe, check that the core temperature is above 205°F (96°C).

Leave the bread to cool on a wire rack.

MAKES 1 X 1 LB 4 OZ (560 G) LOAF

Prep time: 15 minutes
Cooking time: 40 to 50 minutes
Proving time: 1 hour 15 minutes

You will need: 4 ¼-cup (1-litre)
nonstick cake pan

INGREDIENTS

Ingredients for French sourdough
(see page 90)
½ cup (2 ¾ oz (80 g) pitted
Kalamata black olives
2 fresh rosemary sprigs, each
about 4 inches (10 cm)
1 teaspoon coarse salt
Oil for the mold

Olive and Rosemary Bread

Follow the method for French sourdough (see page 90).

After incorporating the yeast, add the whole olives and the leaves of one rosemary sprig. Pulse at low speed for 1 to 2 minutes until you have a smooth dough. Place the dough into a mold, or one brushed very lightly with oil.
Sprinkle over a few grains of coarse salt and place the remaining rosemary sprig on the surface of the loaf, pushing it lightly into the dough.
Leave to prove for 1 hour 15 minutes at room temperature in a draft-free place.

Preheat the oven to 475 °F (240 °C).
Bake for 20 minutes, then lower the temperature to 390 °F (200 °C) and bake for a further 20 to 30 minutes, depending on your oven.

The crust of your bread should be golden and the grains of salt starting to brown.
If you have a probe, check that the core temperature is above 205 °F (96 °C).

Leave the bread to cool on a wire rack.

MAKES 1 X 1 LB (450 G) LOAF

Prep time: 15 minutes
Cooking time: 40 to 50 minutes
Proving time: 1 hour 15 minutes

You will need: 4 ¼-cup (1-litre)
nonstick loaf pan

INGREDIENTS

½ quantity of all the ingredients
for French sourdough (see page 90)
⅓ cup (1 ¾ oz/50 g) dried apricots,
cut in half
⅓ cup (1 ¾ oz/50 g) dried figs, cut in half
⅓ cup (1 ¾ oz/50 g) golden raisins
or currants
⅓ cup (1 ¾ oz/50 g) whole shelled hazelnuts
4 teaspoons (⅓ oz/10 g) flour for the top
of the loaf
Oil for the mold

Fall Bread

Follow the method for French sourdough (see page 90).

While kneading the bread, soak the apricots, figs, and raisins in lukewarm water for 2 minutes.
Drain them in a colander.

After incorporating the yeast, add the soaked dried fruit and stir in for 1 to 2 minutes, until evenly distributed throughout the dough.
Place the dough into a nonstick mold, or one brushed very lightly with oil.
Lightly flour the surface of the loaf to prevent the sugar released by the fruit from coloring the dough while baking.
Leave to prove for 1 hour 15 minutes at room temperature in a draft-free place.

Preheat the oven to 475 °F (240 °C).
Bake for 20 minutes, then lower the temperature to 390 °F (200 °C) and bake for a further 20 to 30 minutes, depending on your oven.
Keep an eye on the color of the surface of the bread: the presence of natural sugars in the dried fruits can cause the dough to change color!
If you have a probe, check that the core temperature is above 205 °F (96 °C).

Leave the bread to cool on a wire rack.

MAKES 1 X 1 LB 7 OZ (650 G) LOAF

Prep time: 15 minutes
Cooking time: 40 to 50 minutes
Proving time: 1 hour 15 minutes

You will need: 4 ¼-cup (1-litre)
nonstick loaf pan

INGREDIENTS

3 ½ oz (100 g) dark chocolate
2 ½ tablespoons (½ oz/15 g)
unsweetened cocoa powder
Ingredients for French sourdough
(see page 90)
3 tablespoons (1 ½ oz/40 g) superfine
sugar (optional)
Oil for the mold

Chocolate Bread

Coarsely chop the chocolate using a knife.

Mix the cocoa and flour, then follow the method for French sourdough (see page 90).
After incorporating the yeast, add the dark chocolate chips and the sugar, if using. Pulse at low speed for 1 to 2 minutes.

Place the dough into a nonstick mold, or one brushed very lightly with oil.

Leave to prove for 1 hour 15 minutes at room temperature in a draft-free place.

Preheat the oven to 475 °F (240 °C).
Bake for 20 minutes, then lower the temperature to 390 °F (200 °C) and bake for a further 20 to 30 minutes, depending on your oven.
If you have a probe, check that the core temperature is above 205 °F (96 °C).

Leave the bread to cool on a wire rack.

MAKES 1 X 1 LB 2 OZ (500 G) LOAF

Prep time: 15 minutes
Cooking time: 40 to 50 minutes
Proving time: 1 hour 15 minutes

You will need: 4 ¼-cup (1-litre)
nonstick cake pan

INGREDIENTS

FOR THE DOUGH
1 ½ cups (8 ½ oz/240 g) gray flour blend
(see page 88)
Scant ½ cup (2 ¼ oz/60 g) chestnut flour,
+ 4 teaspoons (⅓ oz/10 g) to finish
1 ½ teaspoons fine salt
1 ¼ cups (300 ml) water at 100°F (38°C)
1 ¼ teaspoons (4 g) fresh baker's yeast
1 teaspoon olive oil
Zest of 1 untreated orange

FOR THE STARCH SOLUTION
1 cup (250 ml) cold water
½ tablespoon (5 g) potato starch

Chestnut Bread

Pour the flour blend, chestnut flour, salt, and water into the bowl of a food processor fitted with the paddle attachment. Pulse at low speed for 10 minutes.

Add the crumbled fresh yeast and continue kneading for 2 minutes.

Pour in the olive oil and continue kneading for 2 minutes.

Place the dough into a nonstick mold, or one brushed very lightly with oil.

Leave to prove for 1 hour 15 minutes at room temperature in a draft-free place.

Preheat the oven to 475°F (240°C).

Dust the surface of the loaf with chestnut flour: using a sheet of paper as a mask, flour the bread in diagonal stripes and score the bread on this same diagonal.

Bake for 20 minutes, then lower the temperature to 390°F (200°C) and bake for a further 20 to 30 minutes, depending on your oven.

Keep an eye on the color of the surface of the bread: the presence of natural sugars in the chestnut flour can cause the dough to change color!

If you have a probe, check that the core temperature is above 205°F (96°C).

While the bread is baking, prepare the starch solution. In a saucepan, mix the cold water with the potato starch. Bring the mixture to a boil, stirring constantly. Remove from the heat, cool, then chill in the refrigerator.

For a perfect finish, brush the surface of the bread (on its unfloured part) with the starch solution as soon as you take it out of the oven. This will add shine and can be used on any unfloured bread you make.

MAKES 1 X 1 LB 3 OZ (530 G) LOAF

Prep time: 15 minutes
Cooking time: 40 to 50 minutes
Proving time: 1 hour 15 minutes

You will need: 4 ¼-cup (1-litre)
nonstick loaf pan

INGREDIENTS

FOR THE FLOUR BLEND
¾ cup (4 ¼ oz/120 g) rice flour
¾ cup (4 ¼ oz/120 g) potato starch
1 ⅓ cups (4 ¼ oz/120 g) chickpea
(garbanzo) flour
2 ¼ teaspoons (6 g) guar gum

FOR THE DOUGH
1 quantity flour blend (see above)
1 teaspoon (3 g) ground fenugreek
1 ½ teaspoons fine salt
1 ¼ cups (300 ml) water at 100°F (38°C)
1 ¼ teaspoons (4 g) fresh baker's yeast
1 teaspoon olive oil
2 scant tablespoons (⅓ oz/10 g) chickpea
(garbanzo) flour, to finish
Oil for the mold

Chickpea and Fenugreek Bread

Carefully mix all the ingredients for the flour blend.

Pour the flour blend, fenugreek, salt, and water into the bowl of a food processor fitted with the paddle attachment. Pulse at low speed for 10 minutes.

Add the crumbled fresh yeast and continue kneading for 2 minutes.

Pour in the olive oil and continue kneading for 2 minutes at medium speed.

Place the dough into a nonstick mold, or one brushed very lightly with oil.

Leave to prove for 1 hour 15 minutes at room temperature in a draft-free place.

Preheat the oven to 475°F (240°C).

Dust the surface of the loaf with a little chickpea (garbanzo) flour, then score it lightly with a razor blade.

Bake for 20 minutes, then lower the temperature to 390°F (200°C) and bake for a further 20 to 30 minutes, depending on your oven. The crust of your bread should be golden.

If you have a probe, check that the core temperature is above 205°F (96°C).

Leave the bread to cool on a wire rack.

MAKES 1 X 1 LB 2 OZ (500 G) LOAF

Prep time: 30 minutes
Cooking time: 40 to 50 minutes
Proving time: 1 hour 15 minutes

You will need: 4 ¼-cup (1-litre)
nonstick cake pan

INGREDIENTS

½ cup + ⅓ cup (5 oz/150 g) fine cornmeal
⅝ cup (150 ml) boiling water
1 cup (5 oz/150 g) gray flour blend
(see page 88)
1 ½ teaspoons fine salt
⅝ cup (150 ml) water at 100°F (38°C)
1 ¼ teaspoons (4 g) fresh baker's yeast
1 teaspoon olive oil
2 tablespoons (¾ oz/20 g) fine cornmeal,
to finish
Oil for the mold

Corn Bread

Pour the cornmeal and ⅝ cup (150 ml) boiling water into the bowl of a food processor fitted with the paddle attachment. Knead for 2 minutes at low speed, then chill the dough in the refrigerator until its temperature drops to about 104°F (40°C).

Next, add the gray flour blend, salt, and remaining water to the dough in the food processor. Pulse at low speed for 10 minutes.

Add the crumbled fresh yeast and continue kneading for 2 minutes.

Pour in the olive oil and continue kneading for 2 minutes.

Place the dough into a nonstick mold, or one brushed very lightly with oil.

Leave to prove for 1 hour 15 minutes at room temperature in a draft-free place.

Preheat the oven to 425°F (220°C).

Dust the top of the bread with the cornmeal and score the surface.

Bake for 20 minutes, then lower the temperature to 390°F (200°C) and bake for a further 20 to 30 minutes, depending on your oven.

The crust of your bread should be golden. If you have a probe, check that the core temperature is above 205°F (96°C).

Leave the bread to cool on a wire rack.

MAKES 1 X 1 LB 5 OZ (600 G) LOAF

Prep time: 15 minutes
Cooking time: 40 to 50 minutes
Proving time: 1 hour 15 minutes

You will need: 4 ¼-cup (1-litre)
nonstick loaf pan

INGREDIENTS

Ingredients for French sourdough
(see page 90)
1 teaspoon squid ink
½ cup + 1 tablespoon (2 ¾ oz/80 g) whole
shelled hazelnuts
Oil for the mold

Hazelnut and Squid Ink Black Bread

Follow the method for French sourdough (see page 90).

After incorporating the yeast, add the squid ink.
Mix for 1 to 2 minutes.
Then add the hazelnuts and continue to mix for 1 to 2 minutes, until you have a smooth dough.

Place the dough into a nonstick mold, or one brushed very lightly with oil.
Leave to prove for 1 hour 15 minutes at room temperature in a draft-free place.

Preheat the oven to 475°F (240°C).
Bake for 20 minutes, then lower the temperature to 390°F (200°C). Sprinkle the chopped hazelnuts over the top of the bread and bake for a further 20 to 30 minutes, depending on your oven.
If you have a probe, check that the core temperature is above 205°F (96°C).

Leave the bread to cool on a wire rack.

Bakery Pastries

Sweet Treats

Prep time: 25 minutes
Cooking time: 24 minutes

INGREDIENTS

¾ cup (4 ½ oz/130 g) candied ginger
1 ⅓ cups + 1 tablespoon (11 oz/310 g)
unsalted butter, at room temperature
1 ½ cups (10 ½ oz/300 g) superfine sugar
1 ½ cups (5 oz/150 g) ground almonds
3 medium eggs
2 ½ cups (13 ½ oz/380 g) white rice flour
¾ teaspoon (3 g) baking powder
2 tablespoons (⅓ oz/10 g) chopped
fresh mint leaves

Mint and Ginger Cookies

Preheat the oven to 355 °F (180 °C).

Chop the ginger into small ⅛-inch (3-mm) cubes. Set aside.

Place the butter and sugar into the bowl of a food processor fitted with the paddle attachment. Process at low speed for 4 minutes.

Incorporate ½ cup (1 ¾ oz/50 g) of the ground almonds, then add the eggs, one at a time. Continue to mix everything at low speed for 3 minutes.

Pour in the flour, the remaining 1 cup (3 ¼ oz/100 oz) ground almonds, and the baking powder. Pulse at low speed for 3 minutes.

Add the chopped ginger and mint and pulse or stir in using a spatula.

Shape the cookie dough into 2 ½-oz (70-g) balls. Space them out on a baking sheet lined with parchment paper.

Using the palm of your hand, slightly flatten the balls.

Bake in the oven for 24 minutes.

For a crispier result, bake for an additional 2 minutes.

Remove the cookies from the oven and leave to cool on the baking sheet.

Because cookies are not shelf-stable products, we recommend you eat them on the same day to enjoy them at their best.

INGREDIENTS

1 ⅓ cups + 1 tablespoon (11 oz/310 g)
unsalted butter, at room temperature
1 ½ cups (10 ½ oz/300 g) superfine sugar
1 ½ cups (5 oz/150 g) ground almonds
3 medium eggs
2 ½ cups (13 ½ oz/380 g) white rice flour
¾ teaspoon (3 g) baking powder
5 oz (150 g) dark chocolate,
78% cocoa solids
1 cup (5 oz/150 g) raisins
¾ cup (2 ½ oz/70 g) walnut kernels,
chopped

Classic Cookies

Preheat the oven to 355°F (180°C).

Place the butter and sugar into the bowl of a food processor fitted with the paddle attachment. Pulse at low speed for 4 minutes.

Incorporate ½ cup (1 ¾ oz/50 g) of the ground almonds then add the eggs, one at a time. Continue to mix everything at low speed for 3 minutes.

Pour in the flour, the remaining 1 cup (3 ¼ oz/100 oz) ground almonds, and the baking powder. Pulse at low speed for 3 minutes.

Using a knife, chop the chocolate into shards.

Stir in the chocolate, raisins, and nuts. Pulse for 1 minute or stir in using a spatula.

Shape the cookie dough into 2 ½-oz (70-g) balls. Space them out on a baking sheet lined with parchment paper. Using the palm of your hand, slightly flatten the balls.

Bake in the oven for about 24 minutes.

For a crispier result, bake for an additional 2 minutes.

Remove the cookies from the oven and leave to cool on the baking sheet.

Because cookies are not shelf-stable products, we recommend you eat them on the same day to enjoy them at their best.

SERVES 6

Prep time: 15 minutes
Cooking time: 1 hour 45 minutes

You will need: springform pan
about 9 inches (22 cm) in diameter
and 1 ½ inches (4 cm) in height

INGREDIENTS

FOR THE PAN
4 teaspoons (¾ oz/20 g) butter
2 tablespoons (¾ oz/20 g) rice flour

FOR THE CAKE
⅓ cup (2 ¾ oz/80 g) unsalted butter
2 cups (1 lb 2 oz/500 g) crème de marrons*
(sweetened chestnut purée)
3 egg yolks
⅓ cup (1 ¾ oz/50 g) potato starch
3 egg whites

TO FINISH
Confectioners' sugar (optional)

Chestnut Cake

To prepare the cake pan, melt the butter and, using a pastry brush, grease the pan. Then dust the pan with flour.

Preheat the oven to 340°F (170°C).
Melt the ⅓ cup (2 ¾ oz/80 g) butter.
In a mixing bowl, using a spatula, stir together the crème de marrons, melted butter, egg yolks, and potato starch.
Whip the egg whites.
Incorporate the beaten egg white into the mixture in two stages, carefully folding it in to prevent it from collapsing.
Pour the mixture into the pan.
Bake for 1 hour 45 minutes. Check doneness with the tip of a knife. Bake for an additional 10 minutes if necessary.
Remove from the oven and leave to cool on a wire rack.

When the cake is cool, you can dust it with confectioners' sugar before serving, if desired.

* Clément Faugier® crème de marrons is particularly good for this. The brand also guarantees that its products are naturally gluten-free.

Prep time: 20 minutes
Cooking time: 1 hour 15 minutes

You will need: springform pan
about 9 inches (22 cm) in diameter
and 1 ½ inches (4 cm) in height

INGREDIENTS

FOR THE PAN
4 teaspoons (¾ oz/20 g) butter
2 tablespoons (¾ oz/20 g) rice flour

FOR THE FLOUR BLEND
¾ cup + 2 tablespoons (3 ⅔ oz/103 g)
Chambelland cake mix + 1 ¼ teaspoons
(5 g) baking powder
or ⅔ cup (3 ½ oz/100 g) rice flour
¾ teaspoon (2 g) guar gum
¼ teaspoon (1 g) psyllium
1 ¼ teaspoons (5 g) baking powder

FOR THE CAKE BATTER
2 eggs
½ cup (3 ½ oz/100 g) superfine sugar
1 quantity flour blend (see left)
⅓ cup + 2 tablespoons (3 ½ oz/100 g)
butter, melted
3 tablespoons + 1 teaspoon (50 ml)
freshly squeezed orange juice
Zest of 3 oranges

FOR THE ICING SYRUP
¼ cup (1 ¾ oz/50 g) superfine sugar
3 tablespoons + 1 teaspoon (50 ml)
freshly squeezed orange juice

Orange Cake

To prepare the cake pan, melt the butter and, using a pastry brush, grease the pan. Then dust the pan with flour.

Carefully mix all the ingredients for the flour blend. Set aside.

Preheat the oven to 340°F (170°C).
Make the cake batter. Using a whisk, whip the eggs and sugar.
Add all the remaining cake-batter ingredients and mix together using a spatula until the mixture is smooth.
Pour the mixture into the pan.
Bake for 1 hour 15 minutes.

While the cake is cooking, make the icing. Pour the sugar and orange juice into a saucepan, stir, and bring to a boil.

As soon as the cake is out of the oven, brush the surface with this syrup using a pastry brush.
Leave the cake to cool in the pan.

Serve straight from the pan.

Prep time: 15 minutes
Cooking time: 1 hour

You will need: springform pan
about 9 inches (22 cm) in diameter
and 1 ½ inches (4 cm) in height

INGREDIENTS

FOR THE PAN
4 teaspoons (¾ oz/20 g) butter
2 tablespoons (¾ oz/20 g) rice flour

FOR THE FLOUR BLEND
¼ cup + ½ tablespoon (1 ½ oz/45 g)
rice flour
¼ cup (1 ½ oz/45 g) potato starch
¾ teaspoon (2 g) guar gum
1 teaspoon (4 g) baking powder

FOR THE CAKE BATTER
1 lb 7 oz (650 g) dark chocolate,
50% cocoa solids
1 ½ cups (12 oz/345 g) butter
6 small eggs
1 ½ cups (10 ½ oz/300 g)
superfine sugar

Chocolate Cake

To prepare the cake pan, melt the butter and, using a pastry brush, grease the pan. Then dust the pan with flour.

Carefully mix all the ingredients for the flour blend. Set aside.

Preheat the oven to 340°F (170°C).
Make the cake batter. Melt the chocolate and the butter in a bain-marie.
In the bowl of an electric mixer fitted with the paddle attachment, gently mix the eggs and sugar for 5 minutes.
Add the melted butter and chocolate to the bowl and mix at low speed for 3 minutes.
Pour in the flour blend. Mix at low speed for 3 minutes.
Pour the mixture into the pan.
Bake for 1 hour.

Leave the cake to cool in the pan.
Serve straight from the pan.

INGREDIENTS

6 ½ oz (180 g) egg whites
(about 6 medium egg whites)
1 ⅓ cups + 1 tablespoon (9 ½ oz/270 g)
superfine sugar
4 ¼ cups (12 ¾ oz/360 g) shredded coconut

Coconut Rochers

Preheat the oven to 355 °F (180 °C).

Pour the egg whites and sugar into the bowl of a food processor fitted with the paddle attachment and mix at low speed for 3 minutes.

Add the shredded coconut and continue to mix at low speed for 3 minutes.

Using an ice cream scoop, place 2 ¾-oz (80-g) balls of the mixture on a baking sheet lined with parchment paper.

Bake for about 17 minutes, until the rochers are nicely caramelized.

Remove the rochers from the oven and leave to cool on the baking sheet.

They can be stored in an airtight container for up to a week.

MAKES 6 TARTLET SHELLS

Prep time: 30 minutes
Cooking time: 10 to 18 minutes
Resting time for the dough: 2 hours in the refrigerator or 30 minutes in the freezer

You will need: six x 3 ¼-inch (8-cm) diameter tartlet pans

INGREDIENTS

¼ cup + 2 teaspoons (2 ¼ oz/65 g) margarine* or butter*, at room temperature + a little for the molds
⅓ cup (1 ½ oz/40 g) unsifted confectioners' sugar
1 oz (30 g) egg
¼ teaspoon fine salt
⅓ cup + ½ tablespoon (2 ¼ oz/60 g) whole-wheat rice flour
¼ cup (1 oz/25 g) chickpea (garbanzo) flour
¼ cup (1 oz/25 g) ground almonds
2 ½ tablespoons (1 oz/25 g) potato starch

Sweet Tartlet Shells

Place the margarine (or butter) into the bowl of a food processor fitted with the paddle attachment. Soften the fat at low speed, then add the confectioners' sugar. Mix for 6 minutes, still at low speed, until the mixture is completely smooth.
Add the egg and salt and mix at low speed for 2 minutes.

In a mixing bowl, combine the whole-wheat rice flour, chickpea (garbanzo) flour, ground almonds, and potato starch.
Pour all these dry ingredients into the margarine, sugar, and egg mixture.
Still using the paddle attachment, mix everything together at low speed for 1 minute.
Cover the dough with plastic wrap and leave it to rest for either 2 hours in the refrigerator or 30 minutes in the freezer.

Preheat the oven to 340°F (170°C). Grease each tartlet pan with a little margarine or butter.
After the dough has rested, press 1 ½ oz (45 g) of dough into each pre-greased tartlet pan.
To blind bake the shells, prick the dough with the tines of a fork, line with parchment paper, and cover with pie weights. Bake for 10 to 12 minutes to blind bake (as for apple tarts, see page 132), and 18 minutes for complete cooking (as for walnut tarts, see page 134).

* Depending on whether you want a product with or without lactose, you can use either butter or margarine.

Prep time: 30 minutes for the dough + 25 minutes for the filling
Cooking time: 20 to 30 minutes
Resting time for the dough: 2 hours in the refrigerator or 30 minutes in the freezer

You will need: six x 3 ¼-inch (8 cm) diameter tartlet pans

INGREDIENTS

FOR THE SWEET TARTLET SHELLS
See recipe on page 128

FOR THE ALMOND CREAM
1 ½ tablespoons (¾ oz/20 g) unsalted butter, at room temperature
2 tablespoons (1 oz/25 g) superfine sugar
Scant ¼ cup (¾ oz/20 g) ground almonds
¾ oz (20 g) egg
1 teaspoon (4 g) white rice flour
2 tablespoons rum
½ cup + 1 tablespoon (140 ml) whipping cream, warmed to 77°F (25°C)

Almond Cream Tartlets

Prepare the sweet pie crust (see page 128).

Preheat the oven to 340°F (170°C).
While the dough is resting, make the almond cream. Place the butter and sugar into a bowl and mix using a wooden spoon for 5 minutes.
Incorporate 2 tablespoons (10 g) of the ground almonds, then add the egg, mixing at a higher speed.
When the egg is fully incorporated, pour in the remaining 2 tablespoons (10 g) of ground almonds and mix for a further 2 minutes.
Add the flour and mix for 1 minute.
Pour in the rum, then the cream, and mix for 1 minute.

After the dough has rested, press 1 ½ oz (45 g) of dough into each pre-greased tartlet pan.
If you are not planning to fill the tartlet shells straight away, you can store them in the refrigerator, then fill them with the almond cream when ready to serve.
Spoon or pipe about ⅔ oz (18 g) of almond cream into each of the uncooked tartlet shells.
Bake for 20 to 25 minutes. Remove the tartlets from their molds and cool on a wire rack.

You can use this recipe to make raspberry or strawberry tarts: place a spoonful of jam and some fresh fruit cut into small pieces into the shells.

Prep time: 30 minutes for the dough + 20 minutes for the filling
Cooking time: 55 minutes
Resting time for the dough: 2 hours in the refrigerator or 30 minutes in the freezer

You will need: six x 3 ¼-inch (8 cm) diameter tartlet pans

INGREDIENTS

FOR THE SWEET TARTLET SHELLS
See recipe on page 128

FOR THE APPLE FILLING
7 oz (200 g) peeled and seeded apples
(for the applesauce) + 3 small apples
5 teaspoons (25 ml) lime juice
1 teaspoon (2 g) chopped fresh ginger
4 teaspoons (½ oz/15 g) superfine sugar

TO FINISH
1 tablespoon apricot preserves or
1 tablespoon quince jelly diluted in
1 tablespoon warm water

Apple Tartlets

Prepare the sweet pie crust (see page 128).

While the dough is resting, make the applesauce.
Place the peeled, seeded, and quartered apples in a saucepan with the lime juice, chopped ginger, and sugar. Cook, uncovered, over low heat, stirring regularly. When the apples are well stewed but still have some texture (about 10 minutes), turn off the heat and leave to cool.

Preheat the oven to 340°F (170°C).
After the dough has rested, press 1 ½ oz (45 g) of dough into each pre-greased tartlet pan.
Prick the dough with the tines of a fork, line with parchment paper, and cover with pie weights.
Blind bake the tartlet shells for 10 minutes.
When the tartlet shells have cooled, fill each with 1 ¼ oz (35 g) applesauce.
Peel, halve, and seed the three small apples. Cut each apple half into slices and arrange on top of the applesauce.
Return the tartlets to the oven and bake for about 35 minutes, still at 340°F (170°C).
Leave the tartlets to cool on a wire rack before removing them from their pans.
Using a pastry brush, coat the tartlets with the preserves or diluted jelly.

For this recipe, our preference is for sour apple varieties, such as Belle de Boskoop, Reinette, or Topaz.

Prep time: 30 minutes for the dough + 25 minutes for the filling
Cooking time: 35 minutes
Resting time for the dough: 2 hours in the refrigerator or 30 minutes in the freezer

You will need: six x 3 ¼-inch (8 cm) diameter tartlet pans

INGREDIENTS

FOR THE SWEET TARTLET SHELLS
See recipe on page 128

FOR THE WALNUT CARAMEL
Scant ½ cup (3 ¼ oz/90 g) superfine sugar
1 ½ tablespoons (22 ml) corn syrup
1 ½ tablespoons (22 ml) water
Scant ¼ cup (50 ml) whipping cream
1 tablespoon (½ oz/15 g) butter
1 ½ cups (6 ½ oz/180 g) chopped walnuts

Caramelized Walnut Tartlets

Prepare the sweet pie crust (see page 128).

Preheat the oven to 340°F (170°C).
After the dough has rested, press 1 ½ oz (45 g) of dough into each pre-greased tartlet pan.
Prick the dough with the tines of a fork, line with parchment paper, and cover with pie weights.
Blind bake the tartlet shells for 18 minutes.
Leave the tartlet shells to cool on a wire rack before removing them from the pans.

Make the caramel. Combine the sugar, corn syrup, and water in a saucepan and cook over medium heat.
When the caramel reaches 340°F (170°C), turn off the heat and thin it by pouring in the cold whipping cream, then add the butter in small pieces. Stir gently using a spatula until the caramel is smooth.
Return the pan to medium heat and cook the caramel to 230°F (110°C).
Gradually stir the chopped walnuts into the caramel.

Fill each tartlet shell with the walnut caramel. Leave to cool before eating.

Prep time: 30 minutes for the dough + 25 minutes for the filling
Cooking time: 35 minutes
Resting time for the dough: 2 hours in the refrigerator or 30 minutes in the freezer

You will need: six x 3 ¼-inch (8 cm) diameter tartlet pans

INGREDIENTS

FOR THE SWEET TARTLET SHELLS
See recipe on page 128

FOR THE CHOCOLATE FILLING
2 ¾ oz (80 g) dark chocolate,
70% cocoa solids
2 ½ tablespoons (1 oz/30 g) superfine sugar
1 oz (30 g) egg yolk
¼ cup + ½ tablespoon (65 ml) whole milk
2 ½ tablespoons (35 ml) whipping cream

TO FINISH
¼ cup (¾ oz/20 g) unsweetened cocoa powder
¾ oz (20 g) dark chocolate, 70% cocoa solids
Zest of 1 washed organic orange

Chocolate Tartlets

Prepare the sweet pie crust (see page 128).

Preheat the oven to 340°F (170°C).
After the dough has rested, press 1 ½ oz (45 g) of dough into each pre-greased tartlet pan.
Prick the dough with the tines of a fork, line with parchment paper, and cover with pie weights.
Blind bake the tartlet shells for 18 minutes.
Leave the tartlet shells to cool on a wire rack before removing them from the pans.

Prepare the chocolate filling.
Chop the chocolate using a knife. Set aside.
In a mixing bowl using a spatula, mix the sugar and egg yolk.
In a saucepan over medium heat, bring the milk and cream to a boil. Incorporate it into the sugar and egg-yolk mixture.
Pour the mixture back into the saucepan and heat to 180°F (82°C) on low heat.

Remove the pan from the heat and whisk in the chocolate.
Fill each cooled tartlet shell with 1 ¼ oz (35 g) of the mixture.
Leave to cool, then dust the surface of each tartlet with cocoa powder.

Finally, grate large shavings of chocolate and scatter over the top of the tartlets with the orange zest.

Prep time: 20 minutes
Cooking time: 8 to 9 minutes

You will need: 25-cup silicone
mini-financier pan

INGREDIENTS

⅓ cup (2 ¾ oz/75 g) unsalted butter
2 ½ oz (70 g) egg whites (about 2 or
3 whites)
½ cup + 1 ½ tablespoons (2 ¾ oz/75 g)
unsifted confectioners' sugar
⅔ cup (2 ¼ oz/60 g) ground almonds
2 ½ tablespoons (1 oz/25 g) whole-wheat
rice flour

Mini Financiers

Preheat the oven to 390 °F (200 °C).

Melt the butter at 140 °F (60 °C) and leave it to cool.
Whip the egg whites until they form soft peaks.
Incorporate the confectioners' sugar into the egg whites in
two batches, stirring briefly.
Add the ground almonds and, using a hand-held electric
mixer, mix at low speed for 30 seconds.
Pour in the rice flour and mix for 30 seconds.
Gently fold in the cooled butter and mix for 20 seconds.
Pour the mixture into the mini-financier pan cups to two-
thirds full.

Bake for 8 to 9 minutes.
Turn out while still hot and leave to cool on a wire rack.

Prep time: 20 minutes
Cooking time: 30 minutes

You will need: 6-cup silicone muffin pan

INGREDIENTS

FOR THE FLOUR BLEND
1 cup + 2 tablespoons (4 ⅔ oz/133 g)
Chambelland cake mix + 1 ¼ teaspoons
(5 g) baking powder, or ¾ cup
+ 1 tablespoon (4 ½ oz/130 g) rice flour
1 ¼ teaspoons (5 g) baking powder
1 teaspoon (3 g) guar gum

FOR THE MUFFINS
4 oz (110 g) egg (or 2 large eggs)
Scant ½ cup (3 ¼ oz/90 g) superfine sugar
Pinch of salt
¼ cup + ½ tablespoon (65 ml) olive oil
3 ¼ tablespoons (1 ¾ oz/50 g) applesauce
(see recipe on page 132)

FOR THE FILLING
2 ¼ oz (60 g) dark chocolate,
coarsely chopped
9 ½ oz (270 g) organic pears
in syrup, drained

Pear and Chocolate Muffins

In a mixing bowl, combine all the flour-blend ingredients.

Preheat the oven to 340°F (170°C).
In the bowl of an electric mixer, whip the eggs with the sugar and salt at high speed for 5 minutes.
Add the olive oil in a stream, continuing to whisk at high speed, then the applesauce, at medium speed, and finally the flour blend.
Mix for 2 minutes until the batter is completely smooth.

Fill each muffin-pan cup with muffin batter.
Divide the chocolate into six equal portions. Cut the pears into thin sticks and divide into six equal portions. Gently press the chocolate chips and pear sticks into each muffin cup using your finger.
Bake the muffins for 20 to 25 minutes.

Turn out while still hot and leave to cool on a wire rack.

MAKES 20 CRÊPES

Prep time: 10 minutes
Cooking time: 20 minutes
Resting time: 1 hour

You will need: 8 ½-inch (22-cm)
diameter skillet

INGREDIENTS

2 cups (500 ml) whole milk
1 ⅔ cups (8 ¾ oz/250 g) *Chambelland*
cake mix (or a blend of 1 ⅓ cups
(7 ¾ oz/220 g) rice flour,
1 ½ teaspoons/4 g guar gum
+ ⅔ teaspoon/2 g psyllium)
4 eggs
½ teaspoon fine salt
Neutral oil (for cooking)

Crêpes

Set aside 1 ⅔ cups (400 ml) of the milk, then pour all remaining ingredients except the oil into the bowl of a food processor fitted with a paddle attachment. Mix for 2 minutes at medium speed until you have a smooth batter, then gradually incorporate the remaining 1 ⅔ cups (400 ml) of milk.

Leave the batter to rest for about 1 hour at room temperature, covered with a clean kitchen towel.
Add a little more milk to the crêpe batter to make it more liquid if necessary.

Heat a skillet over medium heat and grease it with a little oil.
Pour a little of the batter into the skillet, tilting it to distribute the batter evenly over the whole surface.
When the batter becomes matt, flip the crêpe over and cook the second side for about 1 minute until golden.
Repeat until you have used up all the batter.

Enjoy right away!

If you are going to fill the crêpes, you don't need to flip them: cook them on one side only.

MAKES 1 BROWNIE

Prep time: 20 minutes
Cooking time: 22 minutes
Resting time: 1 hour

You will need: 8-inch (20-cm) square
cake pan

INGREDIENTS

1 ¼ cups + 2 teaspoons (10 ¼ oz/290 g)
butter + 1 tablespoon for the pan
1 lb 6 oz (625 g) dark chocolate,
48% cocoa solids, roughly chopped
10 oz (280 g) eggs (or 5 to 6 medium eggs)
1 cup + 2 tablespoons (7 ¾ oz/220 g)
superfine sugar
⅔ cup + ¼ cup (5 oz/143 g) white rice flour
1 cup (4 oz/110 g) chopped walnuts

Brownie

Preheat the oven to 355°F (180°C).

Melt the butter and the chocolate in a bain-marie.
The mixture should reach 122°F (50°C).
Place the eggs and sugar in the bowl of a food processor fitted with the whisk attachment and mix at low speed for 5 minutes.
Add the melted chocolate and butter to the egg and sugar mixture and mix at low speed for 3 minutes.
Pour in the flour and mix at medium speed for 3 minutes.
Add the walnuts and mix at low speed.

Grease the pan and line it with baking paper.
Pour the cake batter into the pan and bake for 22 minutes.

Leave the brownie to cool for 1 hour on a wire rack before unmolding it and enjoying it cold. Store it in the refrigerator tightly covered with plastic wrap.

Prep time: 20 minutes
Cooking time: 30 minutes

You will need: pastry bag fitted
with a large fluted or smooth tip

INGREDIENTS

FOR THE FLOUR BLEND
1 cup + 2 tablespoons (7 oz/200 g)
fine cornmeal
2 tablespoons (¾ oz/20 g) rice flour
¾ teaspoon (2 g) guar gum
Pinch of salt
½ teaspoon (2 g) baking powder

FOR THE CAKE BATTER
¼ cup (1 ¾ oz/50 g) butter, softened
Scant ½ cup (3 ¼ oz/90 g) superfine sugar
Zest of ½ lemon
¾ teaspoon (2 g) ground cinnamon
4 oz (115 g) egg (or 2 large eggs)

Corn Cookies (Portuguese *Milhos*)

In a mixing bowl, combine the cornmeal, rice flour, and guar gum and stir in the salt and baking powder to make the flour blend.

Preheat the oven to 300°F (150°C).
Melt the butter in a bain-marie, then remove from the heat and whisk with the sugar.
Add the lemon zest, cinnamon, and eggs and continue to whisk.
Pour in the flour blend and mix in using a spatula (or in the bowl of a mixer fitted with the paddle attachment).
When the batter is smooth, place it in a pastry bag fitted with a large smooth or fluted tip.
Pipe the cookies onto a baking sheet lined with parchment paper.
Bake for 20 minutes at 300°F (150°C), then reduce the oven temperature to 245°F (120°C) and bake for a further 10 minutes to dry the cookies without browning them.

Leave to cool on the baking sheet.
These cookies can be stored for a week in an airtight container.

They come from the Porto region, where they are traditionally enjoyed for afternoon tea. Some people like to dunk them in milky coffee or tea.

Bakery Snacks

Savory Treats

MAKES 1 LB 2 OZ (500 G) CRACKERS

Prep time: 30 minutes
Cooking time: 22 minutes
Resting time: 1 hour

INGREDIENTS

2 cups (10 ½ oz/300 g) *Chambelland*
bread mix or gray flour blend (see page 88)
½ cup + 1 ½ tablespoons (3 ½ oz/100 g)
brown flax seeds
½ cup + 1 ½ tablespoons (3 ½ oz/100 g)
golden flax seeds
1 ½ cups (7 oz/200 g) sunflower seeds
1 teaspoon fine salt
1 ¾ cups (420 ml) lukewarm water
3 teaspoons (⅓ oz/10 g) fresh baker's yeast
⅓ cup + 2 tablespoons (3 ½ oz/100 g)
butter, at room temperature
A little rice flour for the work counter

Seed Crackers

Place all the ingredients except the butter into the bowl of a food processor fitted with the paddle attachment. Mix everything together at low speed for 3 minutes until you have a smooth dough.

Add all the butter and pulse at medium speed until the butter is perfectly integrated into the dough.

Cover the bowl with plastic wrap and leave the dough to rest for about 45 minutes at room temperature.

After this resting time, form the dough into pieces of about 1 ¾ oz (50 g).

Dust the work counter with rice flour, then, using a rolling pin, roll out the dough balls to thin circles. The thickness of the sunflower seeds will dictate the thickness of the rolled-out dough, which should be about 1/16 to 1/8 inch (2 to 3 mm) thick.

Prick the surface of the dough using a toothpick or fork.

Stack the dough disks between sheets of parchment paper to prevent them from drying out.

Leave to rest for 15 minutes at room temperature.

Preheat the oven to 425 °F (220 °C).

Arrange the dough circles on a baking sheet covered with parchment paper.

Moisten the dough circles using a water mister and lightly salt them before baking. Bake for 12 minutes, then reduce the oven temperature to 245 °F (120 °C), or open the oven door, and leave the crackers to dry for about 10 more minutes.

Once they are cool, you can store them in an airtight container for up to a week.

MAKES 1 LB 2 OZ (500 G) CRACKERS

Prep time: 30 minutes
Cooking time: 40 minutes
Resting time: 1 hour

INGREDIENTS

2 cups (10 ½ oz/300 g) *Chambelland*
bread mix or gray flour blend (see page 88)
1 ¾ cups (7 oz/200 g) grated or shredded
Emmental or Comté cheese
1 teaspoon fine salt
¾ cup + 2 tablespoons (210 ml) water
3 teaspoons (⅓ oz/10 g) fresh baker's yeast

Cheese Crackers

Place all the ingredients into the bowl of a food processor fitted with the dough hook and mix at low speed for 3 minutes until you have a smooth dough.

Cover the bowl with plastic wrap and leave the dough to rest for about 45 minutes at room temperature.

After this resting time, form the dough into pieces of about 1 ¾ oz (50 g).

Using a rolling pin, roll out the balls of dough between two sheets of baking paper to obtain strips about 1⁄16 inch (2 mm) thick.

Prick the surface of the dough using a toothpick or fork.

Stack the dough strips between sheets of parchment paper to prevent them from drying out.

Leave to rest for 15 minutes at room temperature.

Preheat the oven to 425 °F (220 °C).

Arrange the dough strips on a baking sheet lined with parchment paper and place in the oven. Bake for 20 minutes, then reduce the oven temperature to 245 °F (120 °C), or open the oven door, and leave the crackers until completely dry, about 20 minutes.

If you plan to eat the crackers shortly after cooking, you can omit the drying phase, and simply bake them for 10 minutes at 425 °F (220 °C). The crackers will be softer in the middle, but they won't keep as well. Drying the crackers completely makes them crispier and gives them a longer shelf life.

Prep time: 5 minutes
Cooking time: 20 minutes
Resting time: 1 hour

You will need: 8 ½-inch (22-cm) diameter skillet

INGREDIENTS

2 cups (500 ml) lukewarm water
2 cups + 1 tablespoon (8 ¾ oz/250 g) buckwheat flour
1 teaspoon fine salt
Neutral oil (for cooking)

Buckwheat Pancakes

Pour 1 cup (250 ml) of water into the bowl of a food processor fitted with the paddle attachment, then add the flour and salt. Mix at medium speed for a few minutes, until you have a smooth dough. While continuing to pulse, pour in the remaining 1 cup (250 ml) of water until you have a smooth batter.

Leave the batter to rest for about 1 hour at room temperature, covered with a clean kitchen towel.

Add a little more water to the pancake batter to make it more liquid if necessary. You may need to add up to ⅝ cup (150 ml) more water.

Heat a skillet over medium heat and grease it with a little oil. Pour a little of the batter into the skillet, tilting it to distribute the batter evenly over the whole surface.
When the batter becomes matt, flip the pancake over and cook the second side for about 1 minute until golden.
Repeat until you have used up all the batter.

Enjoy right away!

If you are going to fill the pancakes, you don't need to flip them: cook them on one side only.

Prep time: 5 minutes
Cooking time: 25 minutes
Resting time: overnight

You will need: 8 ½-inch (22-cm) diameter skillet

INGREDIENTS

2 cups (500 ml) water
5 teaspoons (25 ml) olive oil
+ a little for the pan
2 ¾ cups (8 ¾ oz/250 g) chickpea (garbanzo) flour
1 teaspoon fine salt
Salt and crushed or ground black pepper, to serve

Nice Soccas

Pour 1 ¼ cups (300 ml) water into the bowl of a food processor fitted with the paddle attachment, then add the oil, flour, and salt. Mix at medium speed for a few minutes, until you have a smooth dough. While continuing to pulse, pour in the remaining ¾ cup (200 ml) of water and mix until you have a smooth batter.

Leave the batter to rest overnight in the refrigerator, covered with plastic wrap.

Heat a skillet over high heat and grease it with a little oil.

Pour batter into the skillet to a thickness of about ⅛ inch (3 mm).
Cook over high heat until the socca takes on a nice golden color on the underside. Flip and cook for 1 more minute. Repeat until you have used up all the batter.

Sprinkle the soccas with salt and crushed or ground black pepper. Eat while still hot.

Traditionally, Nice soccas are cooked in a wood-fired oven on tinned copper sheets.

MAKES 10

Prep time: 20 minutes
Resting time: 24 hours

INGREDIENTS

1 lb 2 oz (500 g) fresh skinless salmon
½ cup (3 ½ oz/100 g) superfine sugar
1 cup (7 oz/200 g) salt
1 untreated lime
1 ⅓ cups (10 ½ oz/300 g) cream cheese
2 grapefruits
2 untreated Granny Smith apples
10 slices *Chambelland* bread

Salmon and Grapefruit Tartines

The day before, prepare the salmon gravlax. In a bowl, stir together the sugar and salt. Trim the salmon and remove the bones.

Place the salmon in a dish and completely cover with the sugar and salt mixture.

Cover the dish with plastic wrap and leave to rest for 24 hours in the refrigerator.

The next day, rinse the salmon with clean water to remove all the sugar and salt mixture.

Dry it in a clean kitchen towel, then cut it into thin slices. Set aside.

Zest the lime and stir the zest into the cream cheese (without whipping).

Supreme the grapefruit and cut the apples into thin sticks.

Spread the slices of bread with the limed cream cheese then arrange the salmon gravlax slices on top and finish with the grapefruit supremes and apple sticks.

INGREDIENTS

3 cups (1 lb 2 oz/500 g) cooked chickpeas
(drained net weight)
1 generous tablespoon tahini
Juice of 2 lemons
1 small garlic clove, peeled
4 tablespoons olive oil
Pinch of ground cumin
Salt and pepper
3 raw red beets
3 carrots
10 slices *Chambelland* bread
10 cups (7 oz / 200 g) arugula leaves

Hummus, Beet, Carrot, and Arugula Tartines

Prepare the hummus: drain and rinse the chickpeas.
Place the chickpeas, tahini, half the lemon juice, garlic,
2 tablespoons of the olive oil, cumin, salt, and pepper into
a food processor and pulse. Adjust the seasoning to taste.

Peel the beets and carrots and cut them into thin strips. Place
the vegetable strips in a salad bowl and season with the
remaining 2 tablespoons of olive oil, the remaining lemon
juice, salt, and pepper.

Spread the hummus on the slices of bread, add the strips of
raw vegetables and top with a few arugula leaves.

Prep time: 10 minutes

INGREDIENTS

3 cups (1 lb 2 oz/500 g) cooked
chickpeas (drained net weight)
1 generous tablespoon tahini
Juice of 1 lemon
1 small garlic clove, peeled
2 tablespoons olive oil
1 bunch basil
Salt and pepper
2 avocados
10 slices *Chambelland* bread
2 cups (10 ½ oz/300 g) blueberries

Hummus, Basil, Avocado, and Blueberry Tartines

Prepare the hummus: drain and rinse the chickpeas.
Place the chickpeas, tahini, lemon juice, garlic, olive oil, basil leaves, salt, and pepper into a food processor and pulse. Adjust the seasoning to taste.

Peel and pit the avocados and cut the flesh into thin slices.

Spread the basil hummus onto the bread slices, add some avocado slices and top with a few blueberries.

MAKES 10

Prep time: 15 minutes
Resting time: 2 hours

INGREDIENTS

1 lb 2 oz (500 g) smoked haddock
Juice of 4 lemons
15 mint leaves
20 basil leaves
15 cilantro leaves
1 thumb-sized piece of fresh ginger
1 celery stalk
Zest of 2 limes
1 bunch chives
1 ⅓ cups (10 ½ oz/300 g) Philadelphia®
or St Môret® type cream cheese
10 slices *Chambelland* bread

Marinated Haddock Tartines

Cut the smoked haddock into thin slices. Drizzle with the lemon juice.
Chop the mint, basil, and cilantro leaves.
Peel the ginger and finely dice the ginger and celery.
In a bowl, stir together the haddock, herbs, ginger, celery, and lime zest. Cover the bowl with plastic wrap and marinate in the refrigerator for 2 hours.

When ready to serve, chop the chives and mix them with the cream cheese (without whipping).
Spread onto the slices of bread, then top with the strips of marinated smoked haddock and its garnish.

Chefs'

Delights

Pierre Sang (Restaurant Pierre Sang)

From Korea, but French at heart, Pierre Sang Boyer cultivates this dual cultural heritage daily in the kitchens of his three restaurants in the 11th arrondissement of Paris: one on rue Oberkampf and two on rue Gambey. The three restaurants have distinct identities and atmospheres, allowing the chef to fully express his creativity and his unique character. A fervent defender of nature, committed to values of sharing, generosity, and transmission, Pierre Sang makes it a point of honor to cook using only high-quality local produce offered by artisans in his area. He communicates this focus on local produce both to his teams and to the gourmet diners who visit his restaurants to enjoy his bold and innovative dishes with subtle Franco–Korean flavors.

How do you view bread in your cuisine?

I really love bread! For me, bread has a central place in a meal. Indeed, in my restaurants, it's the first thing that the serving staff place on the table: bread with semi-salted Pamplie butter.

Our customers praise us for it and regularly ask us which bakery we use. I've chosen a large French sourdough, which we slice for all our customers. It represents my philosophy of generous cuisine that's about sharing. I seek, above all, to provide pleasure, and I've found that this also involves bread. It would be unthinkable for me to create a meal without it!

How did you hear about *Chambelland* bread?

We've always worked with stores and artisans in the Oberkampf district. We share a lot between "neighbors"; we're all open, curious, and keen to discover new flavors, and we're always visiting each other. When *Chambelland* moved to the end of the street five years ago, it was a foregone conclusion that we'd introduce ourselves to Nathaniel and Thomas and try their products! I immediately loved the original idea of offering bread made mainly from rice. Since then, they've become essential to the neighborhood, and, more particularly, very good friends! Regarding the choice of bread, it's very simple: we make a selection of those likely to interest us, we try them and we decide as a team!

Pierre Sang-style Jambon-Beurre

How do you like to use bread in your cuisine?

I like the bread to be sliced very thinly, which allows me to make small *tuiles*, for example. We put them in the freezer for a while, then bake them in the oven for a few minutes and leave them to dry. I then add them to fish to add crispness to the dish.

A few words about the recipe

I started with the idea of the essential Parisian ham-and-butter sandwich—and revisited it as the "jambon-beurre 2018"! I chose a plain focaccia bread, characterized by its very soft crumb. I attach a lot of importance to texture—in the choice of bread but also in the dishes we serve in the restaurants.

In terms of its ingredients, you'll find the main elements of the famous sandwich: a light touch of butter on the bread, diced toasted tongue, Comté cheese, and some pickles. But it also contains some less traditional ingredients, such as small pieces of Bayard potatoes and grilled onions. And for the final touches: a piquillo-pepper coulis and some nasturtium leaves.

What do you like about this recipe?

Overall, I like its texture. I also really love the grilled pearl onion: cooked on the plancha, cut in half, and served with coarse salt. It's simple, but I love it! And then, of course, I like the mix of styles in this recipe: a French classic revisited with meticulous and decidedly Asian visual appeal!

Julien Boscus (Restaurant Les Climats *)

For Julien Boscus, cooking is a family affair. This chef from Aveyron is the son of a restaurateur and a *charcutier-traiteur* (pork butcher and caterer), but it was his grandmother, herself a restaurateur, who really encouraged his passion. Since then, he has worked with and learned from the best, both in France and abroad—Frédéric Anton, Marc Meneau, Gérard Garrigues, Pascal Aussignac, Yannick Alléno, and Pierre Gagnaire—who transmitted to him values such as attention to detail, meticulous standards, and the importance of good produce, as well as management and communication skills—and, most importantly, the notion of pleasure and making people happy. Julien expresses these values every day at Climats in his contemporary, creative, and gourmet dishes, which are enhanced by a magnificent selection of Burgundy wines.

How do you view bread in your cuisine?

Bread is very important; it's an integral part of French heritage. A good meal is always accompanied by good bread, real bread. Unfortunately, it's more and more difficult to find it. It plays a very important role in my cooking and in my life—and I've always been fascinated by how it's made: I like handling the dough; I love that sour smell yeast has, the whole process of proving, baking, etc., the savoir-faire, the authentic way in which it's made—I'm fascinated by it all. I've had no training as a baker, but one of my dreams would be to open a bakery!

How did you hear about *Chambelland* bread?

Completely by chance! I simply read an article that explained that M. Ducasse had chosen it for his restaurant. I work with Jean-Luc Poujauran for bread, but at that time, we were looking for gluten-free bread to meet a high demand from customers. I made inquiries, went to meet Thomas and Nathaniel, and found everything in order. I get along very well with Nathaniel, the bread is excellent, and their approach makes sense. I'm impressed by their whole way of working, and their bread has the quality and authenticity that I'm constantly seeking. I use their semi-baked breads in my restaurant: I freeze the loaves, and we finish cooking them in the restaurant as soon as we have a request. We get a lot of positive feedback and I almost always give *Chambelland*'s address to customers!

How do you like to use bread in your cuisine?

Chambelland bread is a little extra that we offer customers to accompany their meal. I like to toast bread in my kitchen. I hate throwing food away; I like to reuse bread that we have left over. Usually, I slice and toast it. Then, you can add whatever you want: truffles, offal, or simply use it to accompany cheese or any other snack from the bar menu. Bread is a basic product that may seem ordinary but that offers great opportunities for self-indulgence: toasted bread, butter, and grated chocolate, like my mother used to make when I was a child—simple but spectacular!

Croq'haddock by Julien Boscus

A few words about the recipe

I revisited the idea of the *croque haddock* that I offer at the restaurant, using *Chambelland's* plain focaccia, which perfectly respects the flavors of my ingredients. We simply split the bread in half and toast it a first time, because gluten-free bread is generally moister than sourdough bread. Then we spread it with herb butter on each side. We use very fresh butter from Deleu, in Picardy, to which we add lots of herbs: tarragon, chervil, parsley, sorrel, and dill. Then we place the haddock on the buttered bread and add a good slice of one-year-old mimolette cheese from Terroirs d'Avenir and a few spinach leaves. We put everything back in the toaster, long enough to heat everything well, so the fish is cooked and the cheese melted. As a finishing touch, we add some marinated red onion and grated mimolette.

What do you like about the recipe?

What I like is the little tribute to the North of France, not only in its flavors but in the provenance of the ingredients: the aged mimolette, haddock from Jean-Claude David in Boulogne-sur-Mer, butter from Deleu in Picardy, and then all those herbs that evoke the northern air. The whole thing has a salty, marine, smoky, and, of course, delicious taste.

Olivier Gaslain (Restaurant Le Villaret)

Olivier Gaslain has been the chef at Villaret for almost thirty years. This self-taught cook is passionate about produce, which is at the heart of his dishes and inspires him to change the menus at this intimate and stylish bistro every lunchtime and evening. He seeks to offer a cuisine that is instinctive, diverse, and authentic. Authentic is the word: at Villaret, they do everything themselves, from butchering the meat and preparing the fish to making the pastries. The indefatigable gastronome knows how to win the heart and palate of food lovers, so much so that the chef opened a second restaurant in 2012, L'Essentiel, where he offers dishes that, though simpler, more affordable and with no frills, are always enhanced by this Normandy cook's savoir-faire.

How do you view bread in your cuisine?

Bread is not the most important thing for me: I cook with produce. But I like it when bread serves as a basis for highlighting a particular ingredient. For example, I love to marry it with fish: fried in olive oil and served slightly warm and crispy, bread adds a crunchy taste to the dish, and I like the contrast of textures it adds.

How did you hear about *Chambelland* bread?

It's hard to avoid them: they're right opposite us! We do everything here, from A to Z—except make bread. We were already working with another bakery, but *Chambelland* offer gluten-free bread, and these days we're coming across more and more people with allergies or intolerances. Working with them enables us to meet this particular demand, so we buy bread from *Chambelland* as well as from our regular supplier. And, let's face it, the fact that they're close by is ideal!

Olivier Gaslain's Scallop and Smoked Herring Roe Bruschetta

How do you like to use bread in your cuisine?

I really like using it in the summer. In fine weather, I offer small bruschetta: marinated raw sardines, bread, tapenade, or similar. I also like to serve bread to accompany certain appetizers: I place it across the plate or on the edge to decorate the dish. A slice of pan-fried bread works really well with a slice of Jabugo pata negra and our mushroom and foie gras mousse.

A few words about the recipe

This is a recipe I love making. As I said, I like marrying bread with fish. For this, we use *Chambelland* multigrain bread, which we fry in olive oil, for a warm and crunchy side. Then we top it with a scallop carpaccio and finish with some smoked herring roe and chives. To decorate the dish, we add a few drops of vinaigrette: a saffron vinaigrette and a beet one.

What do you like about this recipe?

My menu changes every day, depending on what I find at Rungis market. So, I offer something different at every service, depending on the produce, which is always fresh and of high quality. These just happened to be the ingredients I had to hand when I was developing my recipe! So, it's a recipe that's in line with what I do every day in my restaurant, that fits with who I am.

David Toutain (Restaurant David Toutain *)

David Toutain fell in love with cooking during an internship at Manoir du Lys. He then went on to learn haute-cuisine values from Bernard Loiseau, Alain Passard, Pierre Gagnaire, and Bernard Pacaud. But it was with Marc Veyrat that he truly developed his identity, his character, his precision, and his technique. For Toutain, who is the grandson of a farmer, working alongside the chef, using produce offered by the land and the mountains, was an extraordinary experience. In 2010, after embracing other flavors in Spain and the United States, the chef returned to France and set up his gastronomic bar, L'Agapé Substance, there. Since 2013, David has been expressing his creativity with innovative and refined dishes in his eponymous restaurant, with its modern decor and warm ambiance.

How do you view bread in your cuisine?

Bread is of the utmost importance to me. In fact, I even devote a special service to it in my restaurant. I offer a set menu, and we serve warm bread, with butter, at the start of the meal. In my opinion, this reassuring moment is essential, both for foreign customers who are here to eat French style and for our "business" clientele, who, by lunchtime, are getting quite hungry and can snack on bread while waiting for their meal to be served. For me, it's really important to provide this moment. Bread is also indispensable throughout the meal: I like to marry it with the dishes. For example, as an appetizer, I offer corn bread with a poached egg, and a brioche with peppers accompanies one of our salmon-based dishes. For a long time, I wanted to make bread here, in my restaurant. We gave up, because it is a very specific occupation, with complex logistics and timings, but we're fortunate to work with two excellent bakeries: Ten Belles Bread and *Chambelland*, for gluten-free.

How did you hear about *Chambelland* bread?

I was lucky enough to be invited to the opening of Plaza Athénée. The bread served at lunchtime was amazing! I immediately asked Romain Meder where it came from. I wanted to meet Thomas and Nathaniel at once, to find out if I could work with them. The next day, it was sorted. Love at first taste! I've always wanted to work with small suppliers whose approach makes sense and is in keeping with our own.

David Toutain's Chocolate Truffle

How do you like to use bread in your cuisine?
As I said, I love bread, and it has a big role in my cuisine. In addition to all these dish-and-bread pairings, we like to work with thin slices of it. We love to simply broil it in the salamander. I've also married it with cod, served with lovage, wild celery, and grapefruit.
For this recipe, we poach the fish, place it on a thin slice of bread, and finish cooking it on the plancha. Cooking it this way ensures that the fish does not spoil and that the bread becomes much crispier!

A few words about the recipe
In winter, I really like working with chocolate. A chocolate dessert is the most comforting thing. For this dessert, I lined the bottom of the dish with a light praline cream. On top, I put a chocolate crémeux served at about 104°F (40°C). The whole is surrounded with a thin slice of chocolate bread that has been shaped around a cookie cutter then dried in the dehydrator. In the center is some truffle ice cream and a slice of truffle, topped with chocolate shavings, pieces of chocolate bread, and hazelnuts.

What do you like about this recipe?
I love *Chambelland*'s very atypical chocolate bread! This dessert has a nice balance: it's delicate, crunchy, and chocolatey—but light. The contrast of textures is also important: hot crémeux, ice cream, pieces of bread, and cream. It's essential that each spoonful delivers something crunchy to the bite and that it melts in the mouth.

Jessica Préalpato
(ADPA—Alain Ducasse Plaza Athénée***—pastry chef)

Originally from Mont-de-Marsan, Jessica Préalpato, daughter of *boulangers pâtissiers*, grew up in a gourmet world. After a literary baccalaureate, she began studying psychology before finally turning her attention to her true passion: pâtisserie. Since then, she has worked in the kitchens of Philippe Labbé, Philippe Etchebest, the Ibarboure brothers, and Frédéric Vardon. It was with the latter that she became pastry chef for the Corfu group, which led to her traveling and encountering new and unknown flavors from around the world. In November 2015, Jessica Préalpato was appointed pastry chef of Alain Ducasse's restaurant at the Plaza Athénée. Here, she offers refined, well-thought-out, but generous desserts with a natural approach.

How do you view bread in your cuisine?

My father is a baker, but paradoxically, I had no intimate connection with bread until I discovered what it's really about, working with our baker at the Plaza Athénée. Baking bread with him, seeing the proving, smelling all those smells, touching all those textures, I found it incredible! There was so much I didn't know! I've become a fan of bread, so much so that I thought a long time about a dessert based on rye and chocolate. It's the kind of dessert that's complicated to create, difficult to find what I was looking for in terms of taste, texture, and sensation.

How did you hear about *Chambelland* bread?

Chef Ducasse was the first to taste it. He really liked their products. Then the executive chef, Romain Meder, went to meet Thomas and Nathaniel. He even had the privilege of visiting their mill in southeast France. The taste, the texture, the approach, their rice-based, gluten-free sector—it's all very interesting and pleased the chefs. This is how the breads arrived at the restaurant. Their products are exceptional; in terms of taste, they have nothing to do with what you usually eat. To follow through with his approach, M. Ducasse even got a cabinetmaker to make a box for slicing the rice bread for Plaza Athénée, inspired by the model at the *Chambelland* bakery!

How do you like to use bread in your pâtisserie?

I'm not particularly used to working with bread in my pâtisserie. But we did take a closer look at it for the Club des Cent, with the aim of offering exceptional desserts. It turned out to be a great experience, particularly one year, when we were able to create something from a beer sourdough: beer ice cream and burned-bread mousse. To make it, we burned the crust in the oven then infused it in hot milk. Once blended and then whipped into a mousse, it had the taste and smell of toast or crispbread. It was delicious.

Chocolate and Coffee from Our Manufacture

A few words about the recipe
We wanted a chocolate-and-coffee-based dessert with a brioche *pain perdu*. Unfortunately, the brioche was not quite what we were looking for. One day, we tasted *Chambelland*'s chocolate and decided at once that it would work well. So, this dessert contains a 75% Java chocolate mousse sprinkled with diced chocolate bread that has been cooked in a pan with foaming butter and unrefined organic sugar; coffee ice cream; and, underneath, a coffee praline composed of toasted almonds, vanilla, coffee, star anise, and caramel. We added a chocolate sauce from the Manufacture, made from just milk, cream, and chocolate. Finally, we invert a chocolate soufflé, made from an 82% chocolate crème pâtissière, mixed with egg whites and cornstarch for a completely gluten-free dessert.

What do you like about this recipe?
I love the dessert's history. In the beginning, I worked a lot with Nicolas Berger, our cocoa-bean roaster. He gave me a taste of the raw chocolate, and then we thought together about creating a special couverture for this dessert, an 82% cocoa couverture. We then had to work with the green coffee that we get delivered to the Manufacture and that's very bitter. It's an authentic, carefully thought-out dessert, each element of which is sourced, which is quite exceptional. I also like this recipe for the surprises it delivers with each bite: you have this very crispy bread, a light mousse with a bitter sauce, then a soufflé and a hot sauce accompanied by a praline that adds zest.
The whole thing is very interesting and fits with our way of creating desserts: we want to surprise the customer with each spoonful.

The authors warmly thank:

The teams at Éditions de La Martinière:
Laure Aline, Valérie Gautier, Céline Grauby, and
Anne-Laure Cognet for their confidence and their
support at all stages of the writing of this book.

Chae Rin Vincent and Louis-Laurent Grandadam
for translating our commitment into words and
images.

Chefs and experts:
Jessica Préalpato, Alain Ducasse, David Toutain,
Pierre Sang, Olivier Gaslain, and Steve Kaplan,
for sprinkling these pages with their knowledge,
their love of food, and their joy-giving recipes.

Gaëlle Bohé and Isabelle Larignon for their
enlightened advice and their careful reading.

Our loyal associates and partners:
Philippe Zambrowski, Stéphane Pichard,
Gianmario Viola, Laura Albini, and Livia Visconti,
without whom this adventure would not have
the same flavor.

The Chambelland teams for their invaluable
involvement, from the rice fields in Italy
to the bakeries and the mill:
Camilla, Pénélope, Olga, Gaëlle, Laura, Elena,
Fiona, Eléa, Monir, Bozena, Isabelle,
Emmanuelle, Mari, Lallie, Margherita, Mélanie,
Tomoka, Catherine, Zineb, Julie, Coline, Emma,
Christophe, Abdelkarim, Nasir, Michel, Stéphane,
Guillaume, Victor, Nathan, Christophe, Lionel,
Gora, and Arnaud. And also Louise, Priscilla,
Lou-Maria, Houda, Émilie, Héloïse, Lucie, Maud,
Noriko, Valérie, Mana, Mina, Maurine, Charlotte,
Georgia, Floriane, Eurialle, Rebecca, Jorelle,
Alina, Alice, Marion, Bénédicte, Mira, Simon,
Thibault, Benjamin, Eddy, Benoît, Oscar, Carles,
Arthur, Grégoire, Martin, and Sébastien.

Finally, thank you to our indispensable, essential,
inspiring, and wonderful families.

Graphic design: Valérie Gautier
Body text English translation: Flo Brutton
Recipe translation: Anne McDowall
Proofreading : Nicole Foster

© 2018, Éditions de La Martinière,
an imprint of EDLM for the original and English
translation 10 9 8 7 6 5 4 3 2 1
ISBN: 978-1-4197-6105-8

Abrams books are available at special discounts when
purchased in quantity for premiums and promotions as
well as fundraising or educational use. Special editions
can also be created to specification.
For details, contact specialsales@abramsbooks.com or
the address below.

Photoengraving: IGS-CP(16)
Printed and bound in November 2021
Legal deposit: September 2018

ABRAMS The Art of Books
195 Broadway, New York, NY 10007
abramsbooks.com

soft dough
crazy dough
buckwheat
Camargue
Libertarian
Bagging machine
Neroli oil
mill
Innovation
chambell's girl
miller
baker
pastry-maker
salesperson
dough cutter-cum-beater
Elisa test
big-bag
French rice center
sticky
coumarine
Syracuse